THE UNIVERSITY
of NORTH GEORGIA

150 Years of Leadership and Vision

Edited by

Katherine Rose Adams | Michael Lanford | Jason Mayernick

UNG

UNIVERSITY *of*
NORTH GEORGIA™
UNIVERSITY PRESS

Blue Ridge | Cumming | Dahlonega | Gainesville | Oconee

Published by:
University of North Georgia Press
Dahlonega, Georgia

Printing Support by:
Lightning Source Inc.
La Vergne, Tennessee

Cover photograph of Price Memorial Steeple by Alyssa Annis.
Historical photograph courtesy of the UNG Library Special Collections & Archives.
Cover design by David Folds and Corey Parson.
Book design by Corey Parson.

Hardback ISBN: 978-1-959203-01-8
Paperback ISBN: 978-1-959203-02-5

Printed in the United States of America

For more information, please visit: http://ung.edu/university-press
Or e-mail: ungpress@ung.edu

UNG
UNIVERSITY *of*
NORTH GEORGIA™
UNIVERSITY PRESS

TABLE OF CONTENTS

FOREWORD

It is a privilege to provide a foreword to *The University of North Georgia: 150 Years of Leadership and Vision*, a book written in celebration of our Sesquicentennial Celebration. The fact that the university has not only sustained for 150 years but also thrived is a tribute to many who came before me.

I joined North Georgia College & State University as president in 2011. Six months later, the University System of Georgia announced a process of consolidating institutions. We merged with Gainesville State College, and the merger was successful, in large part because both institutions were focused on student success, character growth, and excellence. We became the University of North Georgia, which is now composed of five campuses blanketing the northeast region of Georgia and attracts students from most other states and several territories and countries.

There is strength that an institution draws from its alumni base, and UNG boasts a robust group of alumni who have been successful and who choose to help the next generation, including through the provision of scholarships. With this vital financial support for student success, the university continues to attract high-achieving students, many of whom have been chosen for very selective national honors and opportunities.

The authors have done an excellent job of chronicling our institutional journey and the impact the university has had on our communities, the region, the state of Georgia, and beyond. Each author has lent an array of expertise highlighting the interwoven facets of the institution, while reflecting on the university's past and opportunities the future holds.

I would be remiss if I did not note that UNG's campuses, while united under one mission and as one community, are each unique. The Dahlonega Campus is home to our Corps of Cadets, which is integral to UNG's designation as one of only six senior military colleges in the nation; most recently, our corps earned distinction as the top ROTC program in the nation for the fourth time at the international Sandhurst Military Skills Competition. Our newest campus in Blue Ridge has had such impressive growth, coupled with high retention and completion rates through our Blue Ridge Scholars Program, that additional space is necessary. The Gainesville Campus continues to thrive in a vibrant economic and cultural hub, where we have been able to expand degree programs and pathways to completion. Likewise, the Cumming Campus is expanding and focusing on new degree options, giving the students numerous educational opportunities. The Oconee Campus continues its legacy of providing a strong academic background that leads to successful transfer outcomes.

I believe you will find the North Georgia journey intriguing and, hopefully, an example of how an institution can enhance regional opportunities and economic development across multiple campuses with differing histories and traditions within the communities they serve.

As you begin this book, you are in for a treat. The authors have meticulously outlined the vibrant history of an institution that has overcome challenges and yet continuously honors its campus heritages and a core emphasis on placing students first. With these steadfast commitments in place, the University of North Georgia's future is bright.

Bonita Jacobs

INTRODUCTION

For 150 years, the University of North Georgia (UNG) has made a profound contribution to the economic, civic, and cultural vitality of the North Georgia region while sending distinguished graduates throughout the world in a variety of business, education, government, and military disciplines. One testament to the importance of UNG is its economic impact on the state of Georgia. During the 2021–2022 fiscal year, UNG's total statewide output impact was $723 million, a figure $416 million greater than any other institution in its University System of Georgia classification (Humphreys, 2022). As the essays in this volume will illustrate, students, staff, and faculty from departments throughout UNG are consistently engaged in service and outreach to provide support for marginalized communities and encourage greater civic engagement, particularly in rural areas of North Georgia. Moreover, UNG serves as a significant hub for artistic, dramatic, literary, and musical activities, enriching the lives of individuals who reside within the university's 14-county radius. A particular point of pride is UNG's renowned military cadet program, the Boar's Head Brigade, which has trained prominent military officers since the university's inception and has won the MacArthur Foundation Award multiple times for having the top ROTC program among all of the senior military colleges in the United States. In short, UNG has earned its designations as the state of Georgia's Leadership Institution and as the Military College of Georgia through its comprehensive array of programs and activities—and the powerful state, national, and international imprint its graduates have made as leaders in their respective fields.

This volume of essays has been occasioned to celebrate the sesquicentennial of the University of North Georgia. Congruent with its structure, the purpose of the volume is to (1) illuminate the university's past as the second-oldest higher education institution in Georgia, (2) highlight a multitude of university initiatives and activities across all five campuses, and (3) consider how UNG will evolve as an increasingly diverse and inclusive institution that develops a new generation of culturally competent and innovative leaders prepared for the challenges of the 21st century.

Chapters on UNG's Past

The first four chapters in this book examine the history of UNG and the institutions that consolidated to create it. These chapters range from broad historical arcs in the lives of the institutions to the efforts of programs within the university and the impact of one individual on the life of another at UNG. Allison Galloup's "A Brief History of the University of North Georgia" provides an overview of the university's development. Starting with the opening of the North Georgia Agricultural College in 1873 and tracing the growth of the schools until the present day, this chapter highlights the milestones the community passed on its way to the school we know today. Katherine E. Rohrer and Katherine Rose Adams's "Leaving Their Mark: Female Students, Faculty, and Leadership Organizations at the University of North Georgia, 1873–Present" focuses on the roles that women have had as students, professors, and leaders at UNG. This chapter definitively shows that women have been integral to the UNG community at every level from the founding of the university. Walker McCrary and Kelly Britsky's "Athletics at the University of North Georgia" focuses on the success of athletics at UNG and the way that the athletics department has shaped through the decades. Finally, Anna C. Brown's "There Are No Coincidences: The Leadership and Legacies of Lt. Col. Chandler R. Brown Jr. and Col. Ben Purcell" examines the generational impacts that have occurred in the context of UNG's long commitment to military service and excellence in education.

Chapters on UNG's Present

The second section of this volume includes seven chapters that canvass how different departments and programs at UNG strive to achieve excellence in their daily operations and initiatives. One of the most critical developments in the recent history of UNG was the 2012 consolidation of Gainesville State College with North Georgia College & State University. Ken Crowe, Timothy Daniels, Anna Gibbs, Steven McLeod, and Amanda Nash reflect on how the departments of information technology, libraries, and university relations each navigated divergent cultural expectations and norms during consolidation in "Successful Cultural Outcomes from the UNG Consolidation: Information Technology, Libraries, University Relations." Their chapter outlines useful strategies for nurturing an emergent cultural identity that identifies organizational challenges and leverages the unique areas of expertise that individuals from different institutions can offer. Anna Holcomb, Maggie Segnitz, and Janet L. Marling's "Advancing Transfer Together: How Consolidation Brought Together the University of North Georgia and the National Institute for the Study of Transfer Students" elucidates how consolidation contributed to the union of UNG and the National Institute for the Study of Transfer Students. Through narrative perspectives of transfer program planners, staff, and students, UNG's commitment to supporting transfer students and the academic study of transfer is highlighted. In "Fulfilling the Potential of Authentic Community Engagement," Andrew J. Pearl—the former Director of Academic Engagement—shares the five civic commitments established by UNG in preparation for successfully obtaining the post-consolidation Elective Classification for Community Engagement from the Carnegie Foundation in 2020. The UNG Civic Action Plan serves as a roadmap for the creation of authentic engagement between the university and its diverse partners and communities.

Dual enrollment has experienced exponential growth in recent years by helping Georgia high school students earn college credit at virtually no cost. In "UNG's Dual Enrollment Program: Growth Reflecting Institutional Mission of Access," Chaudron Gille, Imani K. Cabell, and Katherine Rose Adams explain how UNG has assumed a leadership role in the field of dual enrollment by strategically establishing strong links with nearby counties and high schools. Through such activities, the authors illustrate how UNG has also remained faithful to its mission of access while upholding academic standards. In the next chapter, "The UNG Honors Program: A Commitment to Student Engagement, Service, and Scholarship," Amy Burger, Royce Dansby-Sparks, Danielle E. Hartsfield, and Stephen Smith explain how UNG's Honors Program is distinguished by its volunteer work geared toward community service and networking. Furthermore, the remarkable achievements of individual honors students, along with descriptions of their impressive research agendas, are profiled.

J. Michael Rifenburg and Roger Runquist's "Serving Students by Serving Faculty: The Beginnings and Futures of UNG's Center for Teaching, Learning, and Leadership" provides a holistic view of the historical, contemporary, and imagined future of the UNG Center for Teaching, Learning, and Leadership. By establishing responsive programming to assist new faculty, constructing a space to champion instructional community, and laying the groundwork for the innovative programming forthcoming, the Center for Teaching, Learning, and Leadership has consistently sought to generate superior support and continued learning for UNG faculty as a top priority in creating a world-class teaching professoriate. The capstone chapter concerning UNG's present is an essay by Keith P. Antonia, Anthony D. Fritchle, and Billy E. Wells Jr. entitled "Preparing Cadets for Effective Global Engagement as Army Officers: Global Military Programs at the University of North Georgia." Antonia, Fritchle, and Wells demonstrate how an enviable collection of programs affiliated with UNG's Corps of Cadets—the Institute for Leadership and Strategic Studies, the Global Military Programs Directorate, formal collaborations with the International Military Academy Consortia, cadet and faculty exchange programs with foreign military academies, and international academic programs—not only offer cadets a transformative educational experience but also serve to broaden their horizons and augment their foreign language skills in a globalized age where cultural competencies and international understanding are critical for effective military leadership.

Chapters on UNG's Future

The third section of this sesquicentennial volume considers how UNG can serve as an exemplar for other regional universities in an age where international education, an institutional environment of equity and inclusion, respect for multicultural populations, engagement with local and regional community stakeholders, and the production of impactful public scholarship are increasingly vital for the continued growth and relevance of higher education. Sheila Schulte and Raghvendra Singh, in "The Future of International Education at the University of North Georgia: Creating a Global Learning Environment for all Students," delineate UNG's strategies to sponsor education abroad, recruit international students, embed global perspectives in curricular and cocurricular activities, and develop sustainable partnerships abroad. Bryan L. Dawson, Efren A. Velazquez, Rebecca Johnston, and Pablo Bueno Mendoza highlight the importance of instilling a social justice and equity mindset throughout the university in "Inclusion Means Serving Our Students and Our Community." The four authors explain how research on the campus climate and the Latinx student population informs university initiatives pertaining to equity and inclusion, as well as faculty development efforts by the Center for Teaching, Learning, and Leadership. Winnifred Namatovu, Olivier Le Blond, and Pablo Bueno Mendoza continue the themes of the previous chapter in "Glows and Grows Promoting Allyship for Marginalized Populations through Organized Multicultural Structures." They detail how university committees are developing organizational structures to both supplement current diversity, equity, and inclusion efforts and anticipate the needs of future generations of UNG students.

Ariel Turner and Bonita Jacobs examine the role and contributions of university presidential leadership in their essay about the "Presidential Leadership of UNG: Building Partnerships to Advance the Success of Students and North Georgia Communities." Through the application of empirical research on university leadership skills, the advances and successes of UNG are presented in the commitment to more than just the university, but also to the future development of growing strong relationships in communities through a reputation of strong leadership. The final chapter by Michael Lanford, "Public Scholarship for Societal Engagement: Envisioning the Future of Research at Regional Universities," delineates a scholarly agenda for the University of North Georgia by contending that public scholarship is vital for UNG to articulate its societal importance to contemporary stakeholders. While arguing that public accountability and researcher credibility are at stake, Lanford also identifies the potential barriers to public scholarship and explains why UNG might be in a unique position to promote innovative and groundbreaking research that can have a measurable impact on the North Georgia region.

In summary, the 16 sundry chapters in this sesquicentennial volume are united by three themes. First, each of the authors identifies singular historical events and institutional traditions that make UNG a cherished environment for so many students, alumni, faculty, and staff. Second, the chapters detail myriad activities, programs, and initiatives that not only sustain UNG through challenging times but also help the university achieve prominence in multiple fields of endeavor. Third, the chapters project UNG's continued growth and influence as it trains new generations of students for leadership in their respective careers and sustains its mission through enhanced engagement with local and regional communities.

Katherine Rose Adams, Michael Lanford, and Jason Mayernick

Humphreys, J. M. (2022, May). *The economic impact of University System of Georgia institutions on their regional economies in FY 2021*. Selig Center for Economic Growth, Terry College of Business, University of Georgia. https://www.usg.edu/assets/usg/docs/news_files/USG_FY_2021_Economic_Impact.pdf

THE EDITORS

Katherine Rose Adams is an Assistant Professor in the College of Education at the University of North Georgia. Katherine received her Ph.D. in Adult Education, where her focus was on the roles, characteristics, and motivations of community leaders/boundary spanners within university-community partnerships. She also obtained an M.Ed. in Human Resources/Occupational Development, a Masters Certificate in Interdisciplinary Qualitative Research, and a B.S. in Psychology, all from The University of Georgia. Dr. Adams has been working in higher education administration roles since 2005 in areas of graduate advising and graduate programs coordination and development, prior to joining UNG in August 2018 as an assistant professor. Katherine became the Higher Education Leadership and Practice (HELP) program coordinator in 2019 and immediately began creating programing for graduate students, such as a grant writing academy, peer mentoring program for adult learners, program workshop series, and more while developing the foundation for dissertation research at UNG.

Teaching in UNG's first dissertation-based doctoral program, Katherine facilitates coursework on higher education leadership, qualitative methodology research, student affairs administration, supporting underrepresented students, high impact teaching, and law and ethics in higher education. Katherine's research interests are in the areas of boundary spanning, community engagement, higher education leadership, and student research communication (Over a quarter of the contributors for this book are HELP students or alumni!). As well, she is an Associate Editor for the *Journal of*

Community Engagement and Scholarship. Katherine was the 2020–2022 Chancellor's Learning Scholar, the 2021 UNG Alumni Association Distinguished Professor, a 2021 Stephens Academy Fellow, and a 2022 Governor's Teaching Fellow. Katherine lives in Athens, Georgia with her husband, Chad, and their son, Seth, where she is active in her community, especially in areas of homelessness and youth mentorship.

Michael Lanford is an Assistant Professor of Higher Education at the University of North Georgia. His research explores the social dimensions of education, with specific attention to equity, globalization, institutional innovation, organizational culture, and qualitative methods. In 2022, his first book, *Creating a Culture of Mindful Innovation in Higher Education*, was published by SUNY Press. Since arriving at the University of North Georgia in 2019, Dr. Lanford has edited special issues on life history methods for *Qualitative Inquiry* and global higher education partnerships for the *Journal of Comparative and International Higher Education*. Additionally, Dr. Lanford has published approximately 30 articles and book chapters for publications such as the *American Educational Research Journal*, *Educational Forum*, *Educational Philosophy and Theory*, *Higher Education*, *Higher Education: Handbook of Theory and Research*, and the *Journal of Research on Technology in Education*. He has received funding to present his research in Canada, Hong Kong, Mexico, Taiwan, the United Kingdom, and the United States.

Dr. Lanford received a Ph.D. in Urban Education Policy from the University of Southern California in 2017, where he was a Provost Fellow and completed a two-year postdoctoral fellowship in the Pullias Center for Higher Education from 2017 to 2019. He also holds Master's Degrees in Higher Education from the University of Hong Kong (2011) and music history from Washington University in St. Louis, where he was a Harvey Fellow in American Culture Studies from 2008 to 2010. For several years, Michael taught undergraduate and graduate classes in world cultures, music history, music theory, and aesthetics at various universities in the Southeast United States. In his spare time, Michael mentors first-generation students, is an accomplished pianist and percussionist, and enjoys a variety of sports.

Jason Mayernick is an Assistant Professor in the College of Education at the University of North Georgia where he teaches courses in foundations and teacher preparation. As a historian of education, he specializes in the intersection of deviance and education in American culture. His current scholarly projects include the organization of LGBTQ teachers in K-12 schools during the 1970s and the educational programs of reformatories and industrial schools throughout the 20th century. His first book, *Not Alone: The First Gay Teacher Groups*, is forthcoming from Rutgers University Press early in 2024. Additionally, Jason has published articles in *Teachers College Review* and the *Journal of the History of Childhood and Youth*, as well as articles forthcoming in *Historia y Memoria, History of Education Quarterly*, and the *New Mexico Historical Review*.

Dr. Mayernick received his Ph.D. in Teaching, Learning, Policy, and Leadership with a concentration in Minority and Urban Education in 2019 from the University of Maryland, College Park. He holds a Master's Degree in Special Education from George Washington University and a Master's Degree in Curriculum and Development from the University of Scranton. Before becoming a professor, he taught at high schools in Washington, DC; Baltimore; and New York City for 10 years. He lives in Alpharetta, Georgia with his husband Jordan, their dog Latka, and an ever-expanding collection of cookware.

The Contributors

Katherine Rose Adams is the Program Coordinator for and Assistant Professor in the Higher Education Leadership and Practice doctoral program at the University of North Georgia. Katherine teaches coursework on higher education leadership theory, qualitative research, student affairs administration, and law and ethics in higher education. Her research interests are in the areas of boundary spanning, higher education leadership, community engagement theory, university-community partnerships, student homelessness, and qualitative research communication. Katherine is an Associate Editor for the *Journal of Community Engagement and Scholarship*.

Keith P. Antonia is the University of North Georgia Associate Vice President for Military Programs and Executive Director of the Institute for Leadership and Strategic Studies. Lieutenant Colonel (Ret) Antonia retired from twenty years of service in the U.S. Army as an infantry officer in August 2001. He is a 1981 graduate of the University of Connecticut, holds a Master's Degree from the Naval War College in National Security and Strategic Studies, a Doctor of Education Degree in Higher Education Leadership and Practice and a Postgraduate Certificate in Transfer Leadership and Practice from UNG.

Kelly Britsky is a 2022 graduate of the University of North Georgia's Doctoral program in Higher Education Leadership and Practice. Her dissertation and ongoing research agenda investigates the role of mentoring in promoting greater equity among college athletics leadership. A highly decorated athlete and coach in basketball, volleyball, and softball, Dr. Britsky has over 25 years of experience in college athletics and higher education. Dr. Britsky was inducted into both the Abraham Baldwin Agriculture College Hall of Fame in 2010 and LaGrange College Hall of Fame in 2013.

Anna C. Brown has spent over fourteen years as a professional at the University of North Georgia. As Executive Director of University Events, she oversees university-wide events and event services for all five campuses. She has completed over 100 commencement ceremonies and supported numerous presidential events. She is a member of the North American Association of Commencement Officers (NAACO) and is a certified Protocol Officer from the Protocol School of Washington, DC. Anna earned a Bachelor's Degree in Museum Studies from Georgia College & State University and a Master of Public Administration from UNG, where she is also currently pursuing her Doctorate in Higher Education Leadership and Practice.

Amy Burger is a 2007 graduate of the University of North Georgia, where she earned a Bachelor of Arts in English and a Bachelor of Science in sociology. During her undergraduate studies, Amy was in the Honors Program. She later earned her Master of Library and Information Science degree at Valdosta State University and her Master of Arts in English at the University of Tennessee at Chattanooga. Amy works as a librarian and instructor of English at Dalton State College. She has been a member of the UNG Honors Advisory Council since 2018, and has been chair of that group since 2019.

Imani K. Cabell is the Assistant Director of Dual Enrollment at UNG and a doctoral student in the UNG Higher Education Leadership and Practice Ed.D. program. Imani's passion centers on eliminating student barriers to a college education and promoting impactful student programs. Her experience working with a variety of students from different high schools and walks of life has enhanced her understanding of program specifications and potential barriers that may impact student success.

Ken Crowe currently serves as Executive Director of UNG's Cumming Campus. As the chief administrator for the Cumming Campus, Crowe works with colleagues across the university to advance educational opportunities and community partnerships. Previously, Ken was the Assistant Vice President for Facilities at the University of North Georgia where he guided a team of professionals providing facility and grounds maintenance across all five UNG campuses, as well as capital planning and new construction management. Prior to joining UNG, Ken worked at the University of Georgia and the Board of Regents. Ken earned his Doctor of Education with a concentration in Higher Education Leadership and Practice from UNG in 2021. Ken is married to Lori Crowe, and they have two adult daughters.

Timothy Daniels is the Head of Technical Services at the University of North Georgia Libraries. He is currently enrolled at Valdosta State University, pursuing an Ed.D. in Leadership focusing on Higher Education. His research interests include leadership development programs for academic librarians, managing organizational change, staff development and core competencies, data governance in higher education, and technology in higher education. Tim is a graduate of Appalachian State University and the University of North Carolina at Greensboro.

Royce Dansby-Sparks is a Professor in the Department of Chemistry & Biochemistry at the University of North Georgia. He has served as the Director of the Honors Program on the Dahlonega Campus since Fall 2019 and Assistant Director for three years prior. He initially got involved in the Honors Program at UNG by teaching honors courses and serving on the Honors Program Administration Committee for the last ten years. He earned his Ph.D. in Analytical Chemistry from The University of Tennessee, Knoxville and worked previously as a physical scientist for the Department of Education and the Environmental Protection Agency.

Bryan L. Dawson is an Industrial/Organizational Psychologist and Professor in the Department of Psychological Science at the University of North Georgia; his research focuses on discrimination, and the attitudinal and behavioral effects of positive and negative beliefs towards women, people of color, and LGBTQ peoples. He also serves as the Principal Investigator for the UNG McNair Scholars Program which provides support, skills training, and research opportunities to help first-generation/low-income and underserved enter and thrive in graduate programs.

Anthony D. Fritchle served as the Director of the University of North Georgia's Global Military Programs Directorate. In 2012, Lieutenant Colonel (Ret) Anthony Fritchle retired after more than 24 years in the U.S. Army as an infantry officer. He is a graduate of Armstrong Atlantic State University, holds a Master's Degree from the Air Force Command and Staff College, and has completed work toward a Doctorate in Management.

Allison Galloup is the Special Collections & Digital Initiatives Librarian at the University of North Georgia. She works to document, preserve, and make accessible the history of Appalachia, North Georgia, and UNG. During her time at UNG, Allison has worked with the Bella Lynn collection, the Oconee Historical Society collection, and the institutional records for UNG. She also serves as the manager of the institutional repository, the Nighthawks Open Institutional Repository (NOIR). She is a Certified Archivist who holds an MLIS from the University of South Carolina and a B.A. in History from Berry College.

Anna Gibbs is an instructor of Health and Human Performance at Albany State University and a second-year student in the Doctor of Education, Higher Education and Leadership Practice program at the University of North Georgia. Anna received her graduate and undergraduate degrees in Exercise Science from Georgia Southern University. She is a certified Exercise Physiologist (ACSM EP-C) as well as a certified Strength and Conditioning Specialist (NSCA CSCS). Her research interests include health disparities and university wellness programming. In her free hours, Anna enjoys spending time outdoors with her husband and golden retriever.

Chaudron Gille currently serves as Provost and Senior Vice President for Academic Affairs at the University of North Georgia, a five-campus university of approximately 20,000 students. Chaudron began her career teaching French and English as a Second Language. She has experience in the areas of curriculum development, strategic planning, accreditation, international education, distance education, academic advising, student success initiatives, and faculty professional development. She has a Ph.D. in French Literature from Emory University and a M.A. in Applied Linguistics and Teaching English as a Second Language from Georgia State University.

Danielle E. Hartsfield is Associate Professor in the Department of Elementary and Special Education at the University of North Georgia. She has served as Assistant Director of the Honors Program since Fall 2020. Danielle earned a Ph.D. in Curriculum and Instruction at Old Dominion University and previously taught elementary school in her home state of Massachusetts. Danielle was named as the UNG College of Education's Fieldale Chair in 2020 for her contributions to scholarship.

Anna Holcomb is a lecturer in the School of Electrical & Computer Engineering (ECE) at Georgia Tech focusing in first-year innovations, transfer student acclimation, and professional and technical communication. Operationally, she serves as Assistant Director for the school's Undergraduate Professional Communication Program (UPCP). Anna has extensive experience conducting research within K-12 STEM education environments and brings this expertise in educational research to her instructional practice. She is currently pursuing a Doctor of Education in Higher Education Leadership and Practice at the University of North Georgia where her research focuses on the experiences of faculty outside the tenure track.

Bonita Jacobs is the 17th President of the University of North Georgia, which serves nearly 20,000 students across five campuses. She is the University's first woman president and is only the second to lead one of the country's six Senior Military Colleges. A recipient of multiple awards for leadership in higher education, President Jacobs is the founder and first Executive Director of the National Institute for the Study of Transfer Students. Jacobs received a Bachelor's Degree in Spanish and History and a Master's in Counseling from Stephen F. Austin State University and earned a Doctorate in Educational Administration from Texas A&M University.

Rebecca Johnston is Associate Director of the Center for Teaching, Learning, and Leadership (CTLL) at the University of North Georgia, where she administers a team of directors and fellows who provide faculty development programming to the university across five campus locations. Rebecca develops and presents programming on a wide range of pedagogy topics, conducts internal assessment, and provides leadership in carrying out the CTLL strategic plan. She serves as chair of the Southern Regional Faculty and Instructional Development Consortium, and her fields of scholarly expertise are affective response to music, quantitative human studies research, and teaching and learning pedagogies.

Michael Lanford is an Assistant Professor of Higher Education at the University of North Georgia. His research explores the social dimensions of education, with specific attention to equity, globalization, institutional innovation, organizational culture, and qualitative methods. In summer 2022, his first book, entitled *Creating a Culture of Mindful Innovation in Higher Education*, was published by SUNY Press. Additionally, Michael has written multiple articles for scholarly publications, such as the *American Educational Research Journal, Higher Education, Higher Education: Handbook of Theory and Research,* the *Journal of Research on Technology in Education,* and *Qualitative Inquiry.*

Olivier Le Blond is an Associate Professor of French at the University of North Georgia. He has published in *The French Review, Nouvelles Études Francophone,* and *Women's Studies International Forum.* He has contributed chapters in *Éduquer en pays dominé* (2019) and *Abdellah Taïa's Queer Migrations: Non-Places, Affect, and Temporalities* (2021). He is a member of UNG's Gender Studies Council and is committed to creating a safer campus for students and faculty of the LGBTQ+ community through his involvement in the Safe Zone Trainings. He served as Director of French and Francophone Studies of NeMLA (2019–2022).

Janet L. Marling is the Executive Director of the National Institute for the Study of Transfer Students (NISTS), where she leads a team committed to ensuring today's diverse mobile learners have equitable and inclusive access to educational opportunities and the ongoing resources needed to achieve their academic goals. As an Associate Professor in UNG's College of Education, Dr. Marling also leads the Post-Master's Certificate in Transfer Leadership and Practice. Her professional portfolio has included executive and practitioner roles in student affairs and enrollment management, orientation and transition programs, personal and career counseling, peer mentoring, leadership, and learning support.

Walker McCrary was with UNG for five years as part of the Department of Athletics' External Operations team as the Athletic Communications Coordinator. He oversaw the department's athletic communications coverage of all 13 intercollegiate sports as well as new media initiatives, including the Nighthawk Sports Network's 100+ annual broadcasts. Walker graduated from the University of Georgia in 2016 with a Bachelor of Science degree in Statistics as well as a Certification in Sports Media from the nationally acclaimed Grady College of Journalism and Mass Communications. He married the former Charlotte Greenway in December 2021.

Steven McLeod is the Associate Vice President and Chief Information Officer for the University of North Georgia. In this role, he is responsible for the computing environment on UNG's five campuses. He is a 2002 graduate of UNG and has worked at the university since 2005. Steven also holds an MBA from Kennesaw State University and obtained his Doctorate from the University of Georgia in 2017. He is a veteran of the U.S. Navy Submarine Force, where he served for 20 years. Steven and his wife Ann reside near Dahlonega, Georgia.

Pablo Bueno Mendoza serves as the UNG Director of Diversity and Inclusion/Chief Diversity Officer since spring 2019. In this role, he coordinates the Campus Climate Survey Team and the Engaging Difficult Dialogues Workshop. He serves as a diversity/equity/inclusion consultant to the colleges and divisions. Pablo is currently serving on the University System of Georgia Regents Advisory Council of Chief Diversity Officers. Pablo has served with the Council for the Advancement of Standards in Higher Education, Greater Pittsburgh Higher Education Diversity Consortium, and the National Association of Student Personnel Administrators IV-West Region.

Winnifred Namatovu is an Associate Professor in the Department of Middle Grades, Secondary, and Science Education at the University of North Georgia. In her role, she teaches undergraduate and graduate students in the Middle Grades and Secondary education programs and coordinates the Master of Education in Middle Grades Math and Science program. Her research interests include creating inclusive learning spaces through practices such as culturally inclusive pedagogy, equity pedagogy, and social justice pedagogy.

Amanda Nash is the Assistant Dean of Libraries at the University of North Georgia, where she leads the libraries' Reference and Instruction division. In addition to reference services and information literacy, her professional interests include library administration, pedagogy, faculty development, and instructional design. Amanda received her B.A. in English Literature from Dickinson College and her MLIS from the University of South Carolina. When she's not at the library, you'll most often find her walking her 60-pound lapdog, Bodhi.

Andrew J. Pearl serves as the Director of Community Engagement Research and Publications at the University of Alabama's Center for Community-Based Partnerships, and as Executive Editor of the *Journal of Community Engagement and Scholarship*. From 2015–2019, he was the founding Director of Academic Engagement at the University of North Georgia. He earned his Ph.D. from the University of Georgia's Louise

McBee Institute of Higher Education, an M.P.A from UGA, an M.M. from the University of New Mexico, and a B.M. from Vanderbilt University.

J. Michael Rifenburg is a Professor of English at the University of North Georgia, serves as Co-Director of First-Year Composition, and Senior Faculty Fellow for Scholarly Writing with UNG's Center for Teaching, Learning, and Leadership. He authored *The Embodied Playbook: Writing Practices of Student-Athletes* (Utah State University Press, 2018) and *Drilled to Write: Becoming a Cadet Writer at a Senior Military College* (Utah State University Press, 2022). He is a recipient of the University System of Georgia Regents' Scholarship of Teaching & Learning Award.

Katherine E. Rohrer is an Assistant Professor of History at the University of North Georgia. Her scholarship explores the intersection of gender, race, religion, and education in the 19th- and early 20th-century South. Her published articles and book chapters include: *Martha Williford Payne's (Re)constructions of Race, Gender, and Southern Identity in Missionary Liberia, 1850-1870; The Lucy Cobb Institute: Mildred Lewis Rutherford and her Mission to Preserve an Idealized Southern Community; Lifting the Veil of Obscurity?: Lucy Webb Hayes, America's First 'First Lady';* and *Slaveholding Women and the Religious Instruction of Slaves in Post-Emancipation Memory.*

Roger Runquist currently serves as the Director for the University of North Georgia's Center for Teaching, Learning, and Leadership (CTLL). Roger joined UNG in 2020, bringing over 20 years of faculty development experience. Roger holds an Ed.D. from Illinois State University in Curriculum and Instruction, a Master's in Industrial Technology, and a Bachelor's in Computer Science. He enjoys collaborating and finding ways to apply innovative solutions to problems.

Sheila Schulte is Associate Vice President for International Programs at the University of North Georgia, and her role is focused on managing the Center for Global Engagement and creating innovative strategic initiatives that promote global learning. She has been at UNG since 2018 and has been an international education practitioner since 1995, working at the University of Idaho, Emory University, Georgia Tech, and NAFSA.

Maggie Segnitz is the Assistant Director of Academic Advising at the University of North Georgia; she oversees day-to-day operations and a team of professional academic advisors on the Gainesville campus. Maggie has extensive experience in the field of academic advising, with a specific focus on academic advisor training, transfer student support, and transfer credit. Maggie is currently focusing her research on academic advisor training on supporting transfer students in the University System of Georgia while pursuing the Doctor of Education in Higher Education Leadership and Practice at the University of North Georgia.

Raghvendra Singh is a doctoral student in the Higher Education Leadership and Practice program at the University of North Georgia. Ragh serves as Program Manager for Strategic Global Initiatives at Northern Arizona University. He came to the United States as an international graduate student in 2006 and has worked in higher education since 2009, working at the State Fair Community College, University of Missouri-Columbia, and Northern Arizona University.

Stephen Smith is a Professor of Psychology at the University of North Georgia, where he has worked since 1993. He earned his Bachelor's Degree in Psychology at the University of Texas and his Ph.D. in Social Psychology at the University of Georgia. He served as Honors Program Director from 2001 to 2019.

Ariel Turner is the Associate Dean for Collections and Discovery at Clemson University. She is a recent graduate of the University of North Georgia's Higher Education Leadership and Practice doctoral program, where her dissertation research focused on the lived experience of women presidents within the Boundaryless Career Competencies. She previously served as Department Chair for Library Resources at Kennesaw State University. Ariel received her Master's in Library and Information Science from Valdosta State University and graduated with honors from Oglethorpe University, with a Bachelor of Arts in Art History and International Affairs. She is currently active as a member of the American Council on Education (ACE) Women's Network for Georgia.

Efren A. Velazquez is an Assistant Professor in the Department of Psychological Science at the University of North Georgia, Gainesville campus. He obtained his B.A. in Psychology from Boise State University, M.S. in General Psychology, and Ph.D. in Health Psychology from Virginia Commonwealth University. His research interests include examining the associations that cultural values and parental practices have with Latinx adolescent and emerging adult health behaviors.

Billy E. Wells Jr. is the Senior Vice President for Leadership and Global Engagement at the University of North Georgia. Colonel (Ret) Wells graduated from Mississippi State University in 1975 as a Distinguished Military Graduate and was commissioned in the Regular Army as a Second Lieutenant of Infantry. He graduated from the Army War College, and has a Master's Degree in Education from Louisiana State University and a Doctorate in Higher Education from Vanderbilt University.

A Brief History of
the University of North Georgia

Allison Galloup

North Georgia Agricultural College: Founding Years

The story of the University of North Georgia begins in 1871 when W.P. Price and 24 members of the Dahlonega community filed the articles of incorporation for the North Georgia Agricultural College (NGAC, 1871). These 25 men sought to take advantage of the Morrill Act, which provided funding for agricultural colleges and universities as long as they also taught military science (Congress, 1871). The state had accepted the money from the act but had not fully developed a land-grant institution that met the requirements. Price saw an opportunity to build a school that could teach primary and secondary education in a region that lacked a public school. In 1870, Price sought to acquire the U.S. Branch Mint building for the new college, though, by all accounts, the building was in substantial disrepair. However, it was being used by a Freedmen's Bureau School, a school for African American children. Price sold a quarter acre of land to the Freedmen's Bureau School to be used as a location for a new schoolhouse (Lumpkin County, 1870). Once the school was built by the Freedmen's Bureau, Price—who was serving in Congress at the time—filed the articles of incorporation and petition in Congress to donate the building and land (10 acres) to the trustees of the school to form the North Georgia Agricultural College (Department of State, 1789).

Once Congress passed the bill giving the land and building to the school, the Board of Trustees, consisting of the 25 men who filed the articles of incorporation, began repairing the Mint and preparing it for students. However, the trustees first had to deal with the issue of funding. With the deed in hand, they petitioned the State of Georgia for a portion of the land scrip from the Morrill Act but found that the money had been promised to the University of Georgia to build their own agricultural school. A small committee of board members met with UGA trustees, and eventually the two groups came to an agreement that NGAC would get $2,000 per year from the land scrip if certain requirements were met. Two major requirements were that the UGA board would approve the college president and faculty members and that the school maintain an enrollment of 100 men (NGAC, Sept. 6, 1872). The UGA board named David W. Lewis president of NGAC in 1872. Their November 11, 1872, board meeting became a momentous occasion when Lewis accepted the job and the board voted to make NGAC the first coeducational college in the state (NGAC, 1872). While the articles of incorporation and requirements from the UGA board do not specifically mention the race of admitted students, Price made a donation of $4,000 and property in April 1873 that came with a deed outlining his requirements for his donations. These requirements included the following:

1. The property is always used by the school and owned by the board or school.
2. The property and money revert to Price or his heirs if:
   a. The building is destroyed and not rebuilt within four years.
   b. The school does not maintain enough qualified instructors to teach 50 students for two years.
   c. The number of students drops below 50 students for two years.
   d. Students of both sexes are not admitted. While the sexes may be separated, according to Price, their education must be equal.
   e. The board, Congress, or the State of Georgia vote or require the school to be a "mixed school for the education of the white and black races."
   f. The board refuses to admit "free of all charge whatever (except for books) orphaned children."

g. The children of Price are admitted free of charge in any department in which the salary of the teachers is paid by the $4,000 donated. (Price, 1873)

Classes at NGAC began in 1873, and by the end of the year, more than 200 students had enrolled (NGAC, 1873). Though it could not award bachelor's degrees, NGAC did award teaching certificates and maintained a primary department. The early college catalogs tout the school's affordability and the benefits of its location. In addition to mentioning the "fine free-stone water" and mineral springs, the bulletins mention two churches, a Masonic Lodge, and a "flourishing Temperance organization" (NGAC, 1873). Though the military science program was not mentioned in the initial catalog, the young men at the school were required to attend drill or parade regularly; also, the trustees decided upon uniforms in the first year of operation (NGAC, January 15 and April 11, 1875).

By 1876, the Board of Trustees was ready to expand the institution's growth. That spring, the board successfully petitioned the Lumpkin County Superior Court for the right to award bachelor's degrees to both male and female students who completed the required courses (NGAC, August 3, 1876). Candidates for bachelor's degrees were required to take courses in Latin and Greek, math, sciences, English, and philosophy. Men were required to complete courses in mechanics and military science. Women substituted French for mechanics and military science (NGAC, 1878–1879). In 1878, the first class to earn A.B. degrees graduated, including the first female graduate, Willie Lewis (NGAC, 1879).

Formation of the ROTC

As a land grant institution, NGAC was required to offer military training to male students and did so from the first year. The early Corps of Cadets was less regulated, as the Board of Trustees worked to find a schedule that both met the requirements and was appropriate for the students. Initially, cadets were not required to wear a uniform, and once the first uniform was implemented, it was neither required nor encouraged. The uniforms that the Board of Trustees decided upon in April of 1873 were "sack coats" in "cadet gray trimmed in black" with a black cap for students who wanted to wear uniforms (NGAC, April 11, 1873).

By 1875, members of the corps were expected to participate in parade or drill once per week on Saturdays at 11 am (NGAC, January 15, 1875). The military courses and corps were under the control of the Board of Trustees and the president of the college for the first three years of the college's operations. In 1876, the board received notice from the federal government that a military officer would be sent to teach military tactics (NGAC, June 12, 1876). Later that same year, the school purchased weapons for the cadets to use; their purchase was on bond, using the college—as physical property—as collateral (NGAC, November 10, 1876). And the U.S. Secretary of War issued the weapons. These weapons were destroyed, however, in a fire on campus in December 1878. After the fire, the Board of Trustees appealed to Congress for monetary support to replace books, scientific and military equipment, and the building that burned in the fire (NGAC, December 23, 1878). It does not appear that the college faced consequences for the loss of the weapons nor did it receive funding from Congress to assist with rebuilding.

Over 40 years later, when the United States was on the brink of World War I, President Woodrow Wilson signed the National Defense Act of 1916, which established the Reserve Officer Training Corps (ROTC). While land-grant colleges like NGAC had an established military program, ROTC formalized and standardized the military programs across land-grant institutions and expanded the training program beyond land-grant institutions (*The Army Reserve*, n.d.). After the National Defense Act of 1916 passed, the NGAC Board of Trustees considered whether the ROTC curriculum should be implemented at NGAC. During a November 1916 board meeting, they determined that participating in ROTC would be beneficial so tasked the president of the college with applying for an ROTC program at NGAC (NGAC, November 8, 1916). The following year, G.R. Glenn, NGAC's president, petitioned the board for permission to "perfect the Military Department . . . in accordance with the Act of Congress of June 3, 1916," thus beginning the process of implementing and further formalizing the NGAC Cadet Corps (NGAC, March 30, 1917).

North Georgia College

The Junior College Years

Twelve years later, at a Board of Trustees meeting, then President John W. West and a group of NGAC students requested the board consider changing the official name of the college, in part to eliminate confusion with the "district's agricultural schools" (University of Georgia, 1928). The board appointed a committee to explore this request, and later, during the same meeting, resolved to change the name to North Georgia College (NGC; NGAC, June 6, 1927). The name change, however, was not made official until 1929 when the Board of Trustees resolved to bring the issue in front of UGA's Board of Trustees, as the college was still under the direction of that board. In the fall, the UGA board secretary began amending the college charter to reflect the new name of the institution: North Georgia College. The name change was made official with the Lumpkin County Superior Court on April 23, 1930 (NGAC, 1930; September 7, 1939). Another possible reason for seeking the name change was the college's interest in joining the Southern Association of Colleges and Schools (SACS), first mention of its "striving for membership" with SACS having appeared in 1926. To meet SACS requirements, the college took the step of closing the preparatory school in 1927 (NGAC, June 3, 1926). The board earnestly took up the question of the advisability of joining SACS in 1928, when President Col. John West requested a meeting of the board to discuss. They formed a small committee to consider the benefits of joining and examine the requirements and what the school would have to do to meet those requirements (NGAC, January 25, 1928). While the 1928 committee seemingly never reported its findings, the board took up the matter again in 1931, forming another committee to examine the feasibility of joining an association of colleges (NGAC, April 25, 1931). At their June 1 meeting that year, the committee reported on the feasibility of joining the Association of Georgia Colleges, the state accreditation body similar to SACS. The committee noted one of the biggest hurdles for membership was professors' salaries, and failure to meet the requirements set forth by the Association of Georgia Colleges in a timely manner would cost the school accreditation. As a result, the committee proposed a four-part plan to meet the requirements without overstretching the college's budget. The plan was to:

1. Only confer A.B. and B.S. degrees,
2. Elect B.P. Gaillard (a long-time professor at the school) as Emeritus Professor of Physics with a salary of $1,200 per year and strict limitations on responsibilities,
3. Appoint a librarian with a salary of $1,200 per year (while this is the first mention of a librarian, the school maintained a small library for students), and
4. Adopt a slightly amended budget for the year 1931–1932 (the amended budget is not included in the minutes). (NGAC, June 1, 1931)

As the board discussed the plan, an amendment was recommended to raise Gaillard's salary to $2,000 per year. That amendment failed, and the committee's recommended plan passed (NGAC, June 1, 1931). The cover of the 1932 bulletin included a note just under the college's name touting their new membership in the Association of Georgia Colleges (NGC, 1932).

While the college was pushing through a name change and working on accreditation, the state was working through a deficit (Pound, 1933). For many years, the Board of Trustees at NGC had noted the lack of funds for basic maintenance and teachers' salaries, even making resolutions and taking votes at meetings on who at the college would be allowed to sign for loans to cover the college's debts. The state began tackling its mounting debts by trimming the budget and reorganizing the executive offices. The education system, according to Merritt Pound, received the biggest overhaul. The Reorganization Act closed one of the state's 27 colleges and dismantled the boards of trustees for every school in order to form instead a single Board of Regents (Pound, 1933). Due to this act, NGC became a two-year school in 1933 (NGC, 1934).

NGC between the years of 1933 and 1946, awarded 1,338 junior college diplomas and offered a "general education and pre-professional program" (Hoag, 1964). By 1941, Chancellor S. V. Sanford touted the school as being the only junior college in the system to increase enrollment between 1940 and 1941 and as being "easily twice as large as any of the other junior institutions" ("Chancellor," 1941). In the same address, Sanford announced his support for building an armory at NGC for the military department.

As the United States prepared to enter World War II, NGC continued to support and grow the military program. In the spring of 1942, the *Cadet Bugler*, the student newspaper, published a brief article about the courses being offered to cadets in preparation for the war. The school prepared students by "going all out for defense with a mental and physical program." It offered both credit bearing and non-credit bearing courses "in this line," including a general first aid class taught by Sara Bruce from the physical education department and evening courses in "hand nursing" taught by Mrs. Scanlan ("N.G.C.," 1942). By fall 1942, Col. C.G. Hammond, professor of military science, announced that NGC would offer a "streamlined" ROTC program. Cadets would begin having drill hours on Mondays and Fridays and would be taught to fire .22 caliber rifles. The military department had also formed "special training platoons" to focus on branch-based training in "close order drill," which ended the traditional Sunday afternoon parade for the corps ("Col. C. G. Hammond," 1942).

On April 10, 1943, the *Cadet Bugler* announced that NGC would become home to an Army Specialized Training Program (ASTP). A group of roughly 300 soldiers were sent to NGC to study engineering, beginning June 14 that same year ("Army," 1943).The soldiers were housed in the barracks, but civilian students and the ROTC continued almost as normal as courses for the soldiers in ASTP were kept separate from the civilian NGC students. NGC taught "special courses" in the dorms for both its male and female students. The college offered female students home economics, typing, bookkeeping, and a specialized secretarial course, and male students courses in aviation, radio, and combustion engines ("Army," 1943). The ASTP program lasted until 1944, when the Army discontinued ASTP in favor of Officers Candidate School ("A.S.T.R.P.," 1944).

After the war ended, enrollment at NGC began to soar. By the fall of 1946, the college had enrolled 700 students and added 12 new faculty members ("NGC Enrollment," 1946). By this time, the Board of Regents had promoted NGC to a senior college again, due to its "outstanding educational work and in order to enhance its usefulness to the state" (NGC, 1946). The announcement of NGC's return to a senior college came in spring of 1946. The next spring saw the first graduating senior class at NGC in 13 years, with three men and three women graduates ("NGC to Grant Degrees," 1947).

Changes and Growth

After returning to the senior college ranks, NGC experienced a period of tremendous growth in enrollment. In 1950, President Merritt E. Hoag wrote in a letter to Governor Herman Talmadge that the campus could not keep up with the growth, declaring that students were sleeping four to a room. In 1964, the school formally requested funding for dorms, an additional dining hall, a student center, and faculty housing in order to accommodate the growth at NGC (Hoag, 1964). Many of these projects were funded in 1965 and 1966 (Board of Regents, 1966).

In the early years of that decade, two African American students, Hamilton E. Holmes and Charlayne A. Hunter, filed a lawsuit against the registrar at the University of Georgia after being denied admission to the University of Georgia (Bootle, 1961). Ultimately, the court ordered UGA to admit Holmes and Hunter. Their admission opened the doors for African American students to attend University System of Georgia (USG) schools across the state. At NGC, the first African American student and cadet enrolled in 1967. In an interview with the *Atlanta Constitution*, a dean noted that the "first black student enrolled . . . producing mixed reactions but no trouble" (Joyce, 1974). By 1974, dorms were also beginning to integrate (Joyce, 1974).

John Owen (1970) took over as president of NGC in 1970 and focused on continued growth. From the beginning of his 22-year term as president, he supported the military program, maintaining quality faculty and staff, raising grades, and increasing enrollment. Owen announced in 1971 that NGC would open its first graduate program, a Master of Education, with the first term beginning that summer.

A major milestone at NGC came in 1973 when women became part of the Corps of Cadets ("Women's ROTC," 1973). The first semester, 11 women enrolled. They participated in drill and took entry-level military science courses. According to *The Bugler*, the women were in a separate company, though they participated in drill without weapons and, like the men, were eligible to sign military contracts and attend summer camp ("Women's ROTC," 1973). The women's ROTC was successful and, in 1977, the Military Committee (1977a) passed a motion to fully integrate women into the Corps of Cadets. The proposal included the requirements for women to be governed by the same regulations as men and for the women cadets to be housed in a single location in a women's dormitory. After this motion passed, the Military Committee (1977b) adopted a standard uniform for the female cadets that included berets, dresses, handbags, hats, shirts, skirts, slacks, and sweaters.

North Georgia College & State University

Under the leadership of President Owen, NGC continued to grow in program and course offerings as well as enrollment. In November 1996, this growth culminated in a new designation for the college when the USG Board of Regents approved a name change. NGC became officially known as North Georgia College & State University (NGCSU) as part of "an effort to bring school names in line with those in other states" (Walker, 1966). At the time, alumni objected to the name change because they were concerned that the new name would shift focus away from the military program (Walker, 1996). This fear, however, proved unwarranted as the school's ROTC program continued to thrive.

As the school moved into the 21st century, leadership initiatives and programs became a focus for the institution. In 2001–2002, a small group of students were the first to graduate with a leadership minor (NGCSU, 2002). That same year, NGCSU received funding from the state and private matching funds to begin developing the school's Leadership Initiative. NGCSU also joined with Gainesville College and the University of Georgia in the Institute of Environmental and Spatial Analysis to start a collaborative program with the Georgia Army National Guard called the NGCSU-Georgia Army National Guard Cooperative Cadet Training Program (NGCSU, 2022). Similarly, academic course offerings were spreading out geographically. In 2002, approximately 7.5% of NGCSU students participated in courses in one of four off-campus locations (NGCSU, 2002). The Appalachian Studies Center was established by grant in November of 2004; in the summer of 2006, NGCSU opened its first doctoral program, the Doctor of Physical Therapy (NGCSU, 2005; 2006).

Gainesville Junior College

The growth NGC (later NGCSU) experienced after World War II coincided with similar growth in the University System of Georgia. With the passage of the GI Bill of Rights in 1944, USG saw an influx of applications and enrollments (Bailey & Paul, 1989). In the late 1950s, it began exploring the potential for a junior college system. By 1957, the state passed legislation setting the guidelines for the junior college system in Georgia (Bailey & Paul, 1989).

Five years later, James E. Mathis Sr., a Gainesville businessman, became president of the Gainesville-Hall County Chamber of Commerce. The same year, James A. Dunlap was named chairman of the Board of Regents. Mathis had a 10-point development plan for the county, with a junior college being part of that plan (Bailey & Paul, 1989). Over the next two years, Mathis and Dunlap worked together to build support for a junior college in Hall County. In 1963, Mathis, who had finished his term as president of the Chamber of Commerce, was chosen to lead the Educational Task Force focused on creating a junior college in Hall County (Gurr, 2014). The task force lobbied for a combined site for a junior college and a vocational-technical school. They based this decision on the Student Interest Survey they conducted as well as on the idea that a combination of a junior college and technical school would better serve the community and boost support for the initiative (Bailey & Paul, 1989; Gurr, 2014).

In March 1964, the Educational Task Force applied for a junior college to USG Chancellor Harmon Caldwell. To meet the requirements of the Board of Regents, Gainesville and Hall County issued a bond to raise $1 million, and local government offered $500,000 to fund the technical institution. An appropriate site also needed to be developed. The regents required a 125-acre site for the school and debated its location early in the year.

They decided on the final location because it was close to a proposed four-lane highway that would connect to I-85 (GJC, 1967b). In the resolution establishing the school, the regents also chose its name: Gainesville Junior College (GJC; Gurr, 2014). After receiving the approval of the Board of Regents, the Educational Task Force began to work on building the campus. On December 13, 1965, ground was broken on the new GJC (Gurr, 2014).

While the site was being decided on and acquired for the college, the Board of Regents began a search for the first president. By summer of 1965, the Board of Regents named Hugh Mills Jr. GJC's president (Bailey & Paul, 1989). An integral part of the college's development, Mills began working to hire staff from his new office in what is now Hunt Tower in Gainesville (Gurr, 2014). Eventually, Mills decided to move his temporary offices closer to the future home of GJC in order to begin building community support and presence in Oakwood (Gurr, 2014).

Finally, in the fall of 1966, classes began at the new GJC, even though the campus was not ready for students. When the first registration was held on September 22, administrative offices for the school were in the Civic Building, and classes were spread between the First Baptist Church and Gainesville Junior High School. GJC also used Gainesville's parks and recreations building and fields, and John Hulsey, a local businessman, hosted the library in his home (Bailey & Paul, 1989).

For those students who registered on that first day, a "temporary paper for a permanent college" called *Challenge* (1966) was available. The paper had information on locations of offices, how students could find where their class would be located, what the responsibilities were for the different departments, and information on orientation and athletics. According to the first paper, 430 students enrolled for GJC's first term ("Welcome!," 1966). Though it borrowed their class and administrative spaces from the city and local churches, GJC developed extracurricular activities in which students participated. The college published *The Anchor*, a permanent student newspaper, and yearbook, and had baseball and basketball teams. A student government, LACOSA, was also founded in that first year (GJC, 1967a).

The permanent Oakwood campus for GJC was dedicated in October 1967; by that time, enrollment was up to 719 students for the fall term of that year (GJC, 1967b). To celebrate the campus opening, a series of events were scheduled for the fall term, including lectures, physical education classes, exhibits, conferences, and television programs hosted by a local channel. With the campus now available to them, student organizations began to flourish. While student government, athletics, and student publications were already in existence, discipline-specific clubs, honors societies, civic clubs, and political organizations were all available for students to join (GJC, 1967).

With the classes underway, a growing enrollment, new campus, and a quality faculty, GJC successfully applied for initial accreditation from SACS in 1968. Two years later, GJC undertook its first self-evaluation for SACS accreditation. After meeting with the evaluation team, SACS ultimately voted to grant GJC accreditation in December 1972; however, they also gave GJC 40 suggestions and 17 recommendations to grapple with over the next five years. These suggestions and recommendations were used to adjust the school's curriculum and administration (Bailey & Paul, 1989).

Gainesville Theatre Alliance

While in the process of becoming accredited, in 1968, Ed Cabell was hired as a drama professor. Cabell, who was fresh from graduate school, created a powerhouse drama program at GJC, and his productions were winning national awards within a year of his arrival (Bailey & Paul, 1989). In 1973, Cabell was awarded the Governor's Award in the Arts by Governor Jimmy Carter "for outstanding service on behalf of the Arts in the State of Georgia" (GJC & Brenau University, 1979). The growth of the program led to the 1979 formation of the College Theatre, a "joint program with Brenau University" (Gurr, 2014).

The College Theatre was a cooperative program that intertwined the drama departments at both schools to create an associate to bachelor's program. Its 1979 press release announced that theatre majors could receive an Associate of Arts in drama from GJC and a Bachelor of Arts in theatre from Brenau. It further explained that courses would be divided between the schools, with Gainesville teaching the lower division courses and Brenau teaching the upper division courses (GJC & Brenau University, 1979). The company would be under the direction of Ed Cabell, with Rick Rose of

Brenau University serving as technical designer. Performances would be divided between GJC, Brenau, and the Georgia Mountains Center Theatre (GJC & Brenau University, 1979).

The College Theatre grew into the Gainesville Theatre Alliance (GTA), which featured local professionals in addition to Brenau and GJC students. In 1990, the group performed the *Scarlett Pimpernel* at the Kennedy Center after winning a national award at the American College Theater Festival (Gurr, 2014). Cabell announced his retirement after the Kennedy Center performance, and GTA selected Jim Hammond as his successor (Gurr, 2014).

Gainesville College

After 18 years of service to GJC, President Mills announced his retirement. In an interview with *The Anchor*, Mills told Susan Stowe he was "leaving because I believe presidents who stay too long tend to drag their institutions down" (Stowe, 1982). After this announcement, GJC formed a search committee, and in early 1983, J. Foster Watkins was interviewed for the position (Bailey & Paul, 1989). Watkins prepared well for his interview, having five initial objectives for GJC. These objectives included streamlining the administration, increasing the visibility of the college, emphasizing professional development for faculty and staff, using the school's funds in a more cost-effective manner, and positioning the college as a host institution for USG in order to draw more resources to GJC (Bailey & Paul, 1989).

Watkins earned the search committee's recommendation, and the Board of Regents approved him as president in the spring of 1983. An inauguration was planned for October 1983, with Watkins assuming his duties as president on July 1 of that year (Bailey & Paul, 1989). In its article about the inauguration, *The Anchor* notes that student attendance at the event was low, but the event "was a great success" (Logsdon, 1983). Upon taking office, Watkins began working his way through the list of objectives he shared during his interview (Bailey & Paul, 1989).

Watkins hired a dean of the college, a position which combined academic programs and student services—previously, these areas were represented by two deans—and eliminated the associate dean position (Gurr, 2014).

Between 1984 and 1986, athletics programs were canceled due to lack of both financial support and spectators, which caused a reevaluation of funding allocations (Gurr, 2014). These funds were reallocated to academic programs. Fundraising was a large part of Watkins's agenda. To raise the college's visibility and begin fundraising, Watkins attended local chamber of commerce breakfasts hosted by the foundation in the college's service area, and an Alumni Association was developed out of a steering committee formed in 1985 (Gurr, 2014; Bailey & Paul, 1989).

The Board of Regents, in 1987, allowed the two-year colleges in the system to drop the words "junior" or "community" from their institutions' names. Seeing an opportunity, Watkins quickly submitted a request for a name change. The board approved, and GJC became Gainesville College (GC) on July 1, 1987 (Bailey & Paul, 1989). By 1987, the college, due to its large enrollment of first-generation students, became eligible for Title III funding. Watkins saw another opportunity for the school and worked with faculty to submit a successful grant proposal. The Title III funding would be used to support "academic and administrative computing," the Office of Planning and Institutional Research, and an expanded freshman orientation program (Bailey & Paul, 1989). Encouraged by the Title III grant funding, the college decided to work toward a matching funds endowment. The campaign, called the 25th Anniversary Endowment Challenge, raised $750,000, which was matched for a total endowment of $2 million (Gurr, 2014).

The 25th anniversary of the college was also the year Watkins started to fulfill his fifth objective for the college: become a regional host institution for USG. In 1988–1989, GC was selected to host a Bachelor of Business Administration and an Associate Degree of Nursing by NGC (Bailey & Paul, 1989). During Watkins's administration, the college saw incredible growth in enrollment, funding, and programming. In a winter 1997 edition of *Anchor's Away*, Watkins (1997) announced that he would be stepping down as GC president to take another position in Alabama.

Gainesville State College

That summer, Martha T. Nesbitt (1997) was named the third president of Gainesville College beginning August 1, 1997. Nesbitt brought change to GC upon taking office. She updated the logo for the school from the anchor logo that had been used since the Gainesville Junior College days to a more modern logo that focused on the bell tower at the school's entrance (Gurr, 2014). She built on the foundations laid by both Mills and Watkins, negotiating for a larger science building that would take the school into the 20th century (Gurr, 2014). She received Board of Regents approval to name the gym after Mills, with a dedication in March 1998 (GC, 1998). That same year, she announced that the administration would be working on a five-year strategic plan called Spanning the Millennium: 1998–2003 (Nesbitt, 1998). The new strategic plan included goals to "increase diversity on all levels," to continue leading in technology incorporation, and to increase scholarships and develop funding sources (Strategic Planning, 1998).

W. Michael Stoy joined the administration as Vice President of Academic Affairs and Dean of Faculty. Stoy worked with Nesbitt to continue GC's growth and academic excellence (Gurr, 2014). In 1999–2000, GC was a Bellwether Award finalist, won a Terry O'Banion Shared Journey Award for Exemplary Retention Programs, and became the first two-year school in USG to establish an eminent scholar chair through a matching funds program (Gurr, 2014).

The college continued its growth in 2001 by opening a campus in Athens, Georgia. The original building in Athens was shared with Piedmont College (McCarthy, 2001). The first year, 250 students were enrolled. That number doubled the second year (Gurr, 2014). In 2003, 1,700 students were enrolled, and the Athens campus had moved to the former Truett-McConnell campus in Watkinsville (Simmons, 2003). Gainesville College continued to excel academically on both campuses, and the administration moved to expand course and program offerings once again. In 2005, the Board of Regents authorized GC to establish four-year programs and change its name to Gainesville State College (GSC). The first new four-year degree was a Bachelor of Science in Applied Environmental Spatial Analysis, followed by a Bachelor of Science in Early Childhood Education and a Bachelor of Applied Science in Technology Management (Gurr, 2014).

After 14 years of service, Nesbitt announced her retirement in 2011 (Duncan, 2011). During her final year, she worked on the SACS reaffirmation and a collaborative project with NGCSU. This collaborative project was the University Center in Cumming, Georgia. The center would be a shared campus offering two-year, four-year, graduate, and professional classes (Gurr, 2014).

University of North Georgia: A Consolidated Institution

The Board of Regents announced in January 2012 that eight USG institutions would consolidate to form four institutions. Gainesville State College and North Georgia College & State University were a part of the initial group of eight. Consolidations were expected to begin almost immediately, with nominations of implementation committees due to the Board of Regents by the end of January 2012 (Duncan, 2011). By the end of 2012, the consolidation was approved by SACS, paving the way for final approval from the Board of Regents and the selection of a president for the institution (Johnson, 2012). The final approval from the Board of Regents came in January 2013; soon afterward, signs with the university's new name were revealed on each of the four campuses (Johnson, 2013). Bonita Jacobs, then president of NGCSU, was named president of the University of North Georgia (UNG) and was inaugurated on April 26, 2013, during UNG's first semester (King, 2013).

Two years after the final approval of consolidation, UNG added a fifth campus in Blue Ridge. The campus initially offered "dual-enrollment courses, a full-time program for freshmen, courses for adult learners and continuing education programs for career growth or personal enrichment" (Times Staff Reports, 2015). After five years, UNG saw a growth in enrollment (14,221 in spring 2013 and 18,782 in fall 2017) and an annual savings of $1 million. The annual savings were put back into the school to increase program and course offerings (Silavent, 2018).

Almost 10 years post-consolidation, UNG has an enrollment of 18,985 across its five campuses. The school has 140 programs of study, ranging from certificate to doctoral levels. UNG students have won 214 prestigious scholarships, including 33 Fulbright Scholarships, three National Institutes of Health Scholarships, one Pickering Fellowship, and three Goldwater Scholars (UNG, n.d.). For the last six years, UNG has been listed on the

Forbes Best Colleges list and was designated as a College of Distinction in 2021–2022.

References

Army Specialized Training Program To Be Installed Here. (1943, April 13). *Cadet Bugler.* University of North Georgia, Dahlonega Campus.

A.S.T.R.P. An Integral Part of N.G.C. (1944, July 25). *Cadet Bugler.* University of North Georgia, Dahlonega Campus.

Bailey, J. B., & Paul, J. H. (1989). *A History of Gainesville College: A Quarter Century of Service* (E. P. Donovan, Ed.). Gainesville College; University of North Georgia Special Collections & Archives, Gainesville Collection.

Board of Regents, University System of Georgia. (1966). *System Summary 1965–1966.* https://dlg.galileo.usg.edu/cgi/ggpd?userid=public;dbs=ggpd;ini=ggpd.ini;action=retrieve;format=.;grid=;rset=002;recno=23

Boney, F. N. (1986). Higher Education In Georgia Prior to 1900. *The Georgia Historical Quarterly, 70*(1), 116–126. https://www.jstor.org/stable/40581472

Bootle, W. A. (1961, January 7). Text of Court Order Admitting Negroes to University. *The Atlanta Constitution* (1946–1984), 6–7.

Chancellor Commends College Assures Aid Armory Project. (1941, October 21). *Cadet Bugler.* University of North Georgia Special Collections & Archives, Dahlonega Campus.

Col. C.G. Hammond Calls for Tough Cadet Corps As ROTC Unit Streamlines Program. (1942, October 6). *Cadet Bugler.* University of North Georgia, Dahlonega Campus.

Congress, U.S. (1871). *The Congressional Globe: Containing the Debates and Proceedings of the First Session Forty-Second Congress; Together With an Appendix, Embracing the Laws Passed at that Session; Also Special Session of the Senate* [Book]. UNT Digital Library. https://digital.library.unt.edu/ark:/67531/metadc30893/m1/518/

Department of State. 9/1789- (Predecessor), & National Archives and Records Administration. Office of the Federal Register. 4/1/1985-. (1789). *Act of July 2, 1862 (Morrill Act), Public Law 37-108, 12 STAT*

503, Which Established Land Grant Colleges. National Archives at Washington, DC (RDT1).

Dismukes, C. J. (1972). North Georgia College Under the Trustees. *The Georgia Historical Quarterly, 56*(1), 92–100. https://www.jstor.org/stable/40579364

Duncan, D. (2011, August 8). Nesbitt to retire from helm at Gainesville State College. *Gainesville Times*. https://www.gainesvilletimes.com/news/nesbitt-to-retire-from-helm-at-gainesville-state-college/

Duncan, D. (2012, January 10). Board of Regents OKs college merger plan. *Gainesville Times*. https://www.gainesvilletimes.com/news/board-of-regents-oks-college-merger-plan/

Gainesville College. (1998a, Winter). Invitation to Hugh Mills Physical Education Complex Dedication. *Anchors Away*. University of North Georgia Special Collections & Archives, Gainesville Campus.

Gainesville College. *Strategic Planning Committee Minutes*. (1998b, April 21). University of North Georgia Special Collections & Archives, Gainesville Campus, Records of the Office of the President.

Gainesville Junior College. (1967a). *GJC Student Handbook*. Gainesville Junior College; University of North Georgia Special Collections & Archives, Gainesville Campus.

Gainesville Junior College. (1967b). *Serving Lanierland* [Dedication Program]. University of North Georgia Special Collections & Archives, Gainesville Campus.

Gainesville Junior College, & Brenau University. (1979). *The College Theatre* [Press Release].

Gurr, S. (2014). *History of Gainesville State College: 1964–2013*. University of North Georgia; University of North Georgia Special Collections & Archives, Gainesville Campus.

Hoag, M. E. (1950, April 22). *Letter to Governor Herman Talmadge* (RCB-30109: NGC General File, 1955–1965). Georgia Archives.

Hoag, M. E. (1964). *A Report of North Georgia College of Dahlonega to the Regents of the University System of Georgia* (RCB-30106: NGC President General File, Hoag, Merritt E., 1956–1965) [Report]. Georgia Archives.

Johnson, L. (2012, December 11). College association OKs Gainesville
State, North Georgia consolidation. *Gainesville Times*. https://www.
gainesvilletimes.com/news/college-association-oks-gainesville-state-
north-georgia-consolidation/

Johnson, L. (2013, January 8). University of North Georgia earns final
approval. *Gainesville Times*. https://www.gainesvilletimes.com/news/
university-of-north-georgia-earns-final-approval/

Jordan, J. (2009, November 14). Gainesville State looks forward to new
academic building. *Gainesville Times*. https://www.gainesvilletimes.
com/news/gainesville-state-looks-forward-to-new-academic-building/

Joyce, F. S. (1974, October 21). NGC Has Changed—and Students Seem
to Like It. *The Atlanta Constitution* (1946–1984), 6A.

King, S. (2013, April 27). New university welcomes first president -
Gainesville Times. *Gainesville Times*. https://www.gainesvilletimes.
com/news/new-university-welcomes-first-president/

Logsdon, G. (1983, October 28). Dr. Watkins Inaugurated. *The Anchor*.
University of North Georgia Special Collections & Archives,
Gainesville Campus.

Lumpkin County Clerk of Court (1870). *Deed for Freedmen's School* (Deed
Book R: Part 2). Lumpkin County Clerk of Court.

McCarthy, R. (2001, June 8). Gainesville College Moving Into Athens
"Mecca." *Atlanta Journal Constitution*.

Military Committee. (1977a). *Meeting Minutes* [Minutes]. University of
North Georgia Special Collections & Archives, Dahlonega Campus:
Standing Committees, Box 2.

Military Committee. (1977b). *Meeting Minutes* [Minutes]. University of
North Georgia Special Collections & Archives, Dahlonega Campus:
Standing Committees, Box 2.

Nesbitt, M. T. (1997, Summer). Anticipation. *Anchors Away*. University of
North Georgia Special Collections & Archives, Gainesville Campus.

Nesbitt, M. T. (1998). President's Message. In *Gainesville College 1997
Annual Report and Honor Roll*. Gainesville College; University of
North Georgia Special Collections & Archives, Gainesville Campus.

NGC Enrollment is at Peak; Twelve New Faculty Members. (1946,

November 2). *The Cadet Bugler.* Special Collections & Archives, University of North Georgia, Dahlonega Campus. https://archive.org/details/cadetbugler194211219nort/page/142/mode/2up?view=theater

NGC to Grant Degrees for First Time in 14 Years. (1947, April 15). *Cadet Bugler.*

N.G.C. Trains Students for War. (1942, April 7). *Cadet Bugler.* University of North Georgia, Dahlonega Campus.

North Georgia Agricultural College. (1871). *North Georgia Agricultural College Board of Trustees Minutes, 1871–1896.*

North Georgia Agricultural College. (1906). *North Georgia Agricultural College Board of Trustees Minutes, 1906–1931.* University of North Georgia Special Collections & Archives, Dahlonega Campus.

North Georgia Agricultural College. (1873). *North Georgia College Undergraduate Bulletin 1873.* University of North Georgia Special Collections & Archives, Dahlonega Campus.

North Georgia Agricultural College. (1878). *North Georgia College Undergraduate Bulletin 1878.* University of North Georgia Special Collections & Archives, Dahlonega Campus.

North Georgia Agricultural College. (1879). *North Georgia College Undergraduate Bulletin 1879.* University of North Georgia Special Collections & Archives, Dahlonega Campus.

North Georgia College. (1932). *North Georgia College Undergraduate Bulletin 1932.* University of North Georgia Special Collections & Archives, Dahlonega Campus.

North Georgia College. (1934). *North Georgia College Undergraduate Bulletin 1934.* University of North Georgia Special Collections & Archives, Dahlonega Campus.

North Georgia College. (1946). *North Georgia College Undergraduate Bulletin 1946.* University of North Georgia Special Collections & Archives, Dahlonega Campus.

North Georgia College & State University. (2002). *President's Report.* North Georgia College & State University; University of North Georgia Special Collections & Archives, Dahlonega Campus.

North Georgia College & State University. (2005). *President's Report.*

North Georgia College & State University; University of North
Georgia Special Collections & Archives, Dahlonega Campus.

North Georgia College & State University. (2006). *President's Report.*
North Georgia College & State University; University of North
Georgia Special Collections & Archives, Dahlonega Campus.

Owen, J. H. (1970). *Faculty Meeting Minutes, Sept. 19, 1970* (John
H. Owen Collection, Scrapbooks, Box 9, Folder 1) [Scrapbook].
University of North Georgia Special Collections & Archives.

Owen, J. H. (1971). *College Announces Graduate Program* [Scrapbook].
John H. Owen Collection, Scrapbooks, Box 9, Folder 2.

Pound, M. B. (1933). A Descriptive Account of Reorganization in
Georgia. *Proceedings of the Annual Session (Southern Political Science
Association), 6,* 11–17. https://www.jstor.org/stable/43945691

Price, W. P. (1873). *Deed of Gift for Property and Funds* (Deed Record
Book R, Part 2, 1870–1875). Dahlonega Superior Court.

Silavent, J. (2018, January 10). UNG touts growth 5 years after merger.
Gainesville Times. https://www.gainesvilletimes.com/news/ung-touts-
growth-5-years-after-merger/

Simmons, K. (2003, June 12). 600 Take College Classes At Rural Sites\4-
Year Schools Use 2-Year Institutions To Offer Courses. *The Atlanta
Journal-Constitution.*

Stowe, S. (1982, November 19). Dr. Mills Retires. *The Anchor.* University
of North Georgia Special Collections & Archives, Gainesville
Campus.

*The Army Reserve Officers' Training Corps: A Hundred Years Old and
Still Going Strong—The Campaign for the National Museum of the
United States Army.* (n.d.). Retrieved April 23, 2022, from https://
armyhistory.org/army-reserve-officers-training-corps-hundred-years-
old-still-going-strong/

Times Staff Reports. (2015, August 13). University of North Georgia
opens new campus in Blue Ridge. *Gainesville Times.* https://www.
gainesvilletimes.com/news/university-of-north-georgia-opens-new-
campus-in-blue-ridge/

University of Georgia Board of Trustees. (1928). *Report of the Chairman of the Board of Trustees, North Georgia Agricultural College* (University of Georgia Board of Trustees correspondence and reports). University of Georgia.

University of North Georgia. (n.d.). *UNG Points of Pride.* University of North Georgia. Retrieved May 1, 2022, from https://ung.edu/news/points-of-pride.php

Walker, R. (1996, November 14). Regents approve new names for 3 state schools. *The Atlanta Journal-Constitution*, D.06. https://www.proquest.com/docview/293257593/abstract/3B95E37AFA694319PQ/1

Watkins, J. F. (1997, Winter). President Watkins Accepts Alabama Position. *Anchors Away.* University of North Georgia Special Collections & Archives, Gainesville Campus.

Welcome! (1966, September 22). *Challenge.* University of North Georgia Special Collections & Archives, Gainesville Campus.

Women's ROTC Enrolls Eleven. (1973, October 20). *The Bugler.* University of North Georgia Special Collections & Archives, Dahlonega Campus.

(1966, September 22). *Challenge.* University of North Georgia Special Collections & Archives, Gainesville Campus.

Leaving Their Mark: Female Students, Faculty, and Leadership Organizations at the University of North Georgia, 1873–Present

Katherine E. Rohrer and Katherine Rose Adams

Students

Incorporated in 1871, North Georgia Agricultural College (NGAC), a branch of the University of Georgia, opened its doors in 1873 and provided an education to enrollees at no cost (North Georgia Agricultural College, 1874). During that first academic year, the fledgling NGAC welcomed 98 men and 79 women (North Georgia Agricultural College, 1874). Among those women was Willie B. Lewis, the daughter of the institution's president, David W. Lewis. In 1878, Willie Lewis graduated from NGAC. She was just one of 10 graduates—and the only woman—in NGAC's first graduating class (North Georgia Agricultural College, 1879). Notably, NGAC opened as the first coeducational institution of higher education in the state as well as the South. No other public institution of higher education in Georgia would offer admission to women until the late 1880s. Georgia Normal and Industrial College in Milledgeville was chartered as a female-only institution in 1889, while State Normal School in Athens was established as a coeducational institution in 1891. Women were not admitted at the University of Georgia until 1918 (Boney, 2000).

During its first 20 years, NGAC functioned more as a preparatory academy than a university. Reminiscent of antebellum institutions, NGAC offered traditional coursework that would prepare students to apply to the Georgia College of Agriculture and Mechanical Arts (part of the University of Georgia). Given its purpose as a preparatory institution, few students graduated with a bachelor's degree from NGAC before 1890. Sometimes as few as three graduated in any given year, although at least five women received degrees between 1878 and 1890 (NGAC, 1891). NGAC required all students to take coursework in Latin, Greek, English literature, history, natural sciences, theoretical mathematics, and philosophy (NGAC, 1891). Notably, this curriculum was identical for male and female students, although military duty was obligatory for the former, as stipulated by the Morrill Land Act. Despite its name, NGAC did not provide substantive coursework in the agricultural sciences until the last decade of the 19th century (NGAC, 1899).

Starting in 1878, NGAC granted teachers' licenses (NGAC, 1879). This was likely a response to the growing demand for teachers resulting from the 1868 Georgia constitution, which called for "a thorough system of general education, to be forever free to all children of the State" (Mewborn, 2004, para 3). While financial distress limited public school expansion during the painful years of Reconstruction, interest and resources invested in public education accelerated by the later 1870s and beyond. By 1890, approximately 650 men and women had earned a teacher's license at NGAC (NGAC, 1891). Alumnae of NGAC filled countless positions at public schools in the North Georgia region, collectively instructing thousands of area residents who, before this time, had not been afforded the opportunity of a public education.

By the last decade of the 19th century, NGAC embraced a more modern and well-rounded educational model. Instruction in art, music, elocution, and business expanded. Complementing this time when women were entering the workforce and adopting more public roles in church and civic organizations, NGAC encouraged female students to enroll in penmanship, correspondence, shorthand, bookkeeping, and typewriting classes (NGAC, 1896). Concurrently, the institution began graduating a dozen to a few dozen students each year, and women constituted nearly 20% of all graduates during the very late 19th and early 20th centuries. Female students were recipients of teachers' licenses, certificates of proficiency, and bachelor's degrees. While on campus, they wore uniforms that consisted of a navy blue Eton suit and navy blue cap (NGAC, 1898).

During the late 1890s, NGAC constructed a dormitory that could accommodate 40 women and was under the direction of Mary E. Smith, principal in the female department and an instructress of English (North Georgia Agricultural College, 1901). NGAC reinforced a conservative Victorian culture that, among other restrictions, kept the sexes largely separate outside of formal instruction. For example, female students were required to remain in their room "when not attending recitations" and could not entertain male visitors (NGAC, 1896, p. 31). The town of Dahlonega likewise prohibited the sale of "spiritous liquors" within a three-mile radius, while NGAC forbade students from leaving town without written permission and required that all students—male and female—attend weekly services at either the local Baptist or Methodist Church (NGAC, 1898, p. 8). This begs the question: what activities *did* NGAC students engage in outside of class? During the 19th century, literary societies were omnipresent social organizations on American college campuses. Despite the name, literary societies typically were not literary in nature; rather, they operated as the precursors of college fraternities and sororities. Almost every NGAC student participated in a literary society. An 1890 NGAC bulletin reveals two such societies on campus open to men, while women could join Corona Hederae. Female members of Corona Hederae met each Monday evening from 8 pm to midnight. They engaged in "heated debates" among themselves and periodically opened their debates to the public (North Georgia Agricultural College, 1891, p. 23). Likewise, a handful of women assumed positions as officers—typically as secretaries, treasurers, or "poetesses"—in their respective classes.

The curriculum at NGAC continued to expand during the early 20th century. Ironically, with this expansion in course offerings came even greater segregation of the sexes. For example, for men, NGAC steadily augmented its coursework in agriculture and added a department of electrical and mining engineering in 1904. For women, it established a dressmaking department in 1905 and a domestic science department (which included an emphasis on cooking) in 1906 (NGAC, 1906). Specific to the former, some female students sought a certificate in dressmaking that required three years of instruction, including one year in plain sewing, one year in the drafting of patterns and the making of garments, and a final year of tailoring and advanced dressmaking. Undoubtedly, women gravitated to domestic science, the arts, normal, and business/secretarial classes at NGAC during the early 20th century, purposely pursuing a curriculum that would prepare them to enter the workforce—presumably only until marriage—or for lives as competent, skilled housewives. Outside of the classroom, female students pursued a wider range of extracurricular activities than did their predecessors. Most notably, women's athletics grew more visible at NGAC. For example, women joined the tennis team as well as multiple basketball teams. Other clubs and societies available to women included the Athenian Sorority, *Cyclops* (the NGAC yearbook), the Young Women's Christian Association (YWCA), dramatics, and music (Cyclops, 1915).

The Georgia General Assembly integrated all state-supported institutions of higher learning into the University System of Georgia in 1932 (Fincher, 2005). Georgia and the rest of the nation were in the throes of the Great Depression during the early 1930s. USG, in particular, instituted drastic measures—including closure of several institutions—in an effort to conserve money. Specific to the now called North Georgia College (NGC), USG reorganized NGC as a liberal arts junior college, though the institution was permitted to retain its military program (Roberts, 1998). Consequently, course offerings and certificates were condensed or even eliminated, and the curriculum grew more standardized. Although its identity was certainly in flux, NGC remained committed to offering students an affordable education. Students did not pay tuition, and a 1931 NGC bulletin boasted that the total cost for board, room, and academic fees for in-state students did not exceed 20 dollars per month (NGC, 1931). NGC even maintained a dairy, gardens, farm, and orchard, all of which kept food costs low for students (NGC, 1931).

To earn the state junior college certificate, women were required to take two years of physical education plus 18 courses spread among English, social science, mathematics, biological science, physical science, and French, as well as a concentration of choice referred to as an "elective sequence" (NGC, 1933). Women students still could enroll in more gender-specific coursework in home economics, secretarial science, and education, though courses were limited in depth and breadth compared to what they had been before the Depression. Women constituted approximately 30% of the student body during the 1930s, a time when the total student population hovered between 400 and 500 students. Female students—including many married women—were particularly well represented during the summer term; some years, women represented nearly 70% of the total. On the whole, women participated in comparable extracurricular activities during the 1930s to those during the 1920s. Entertainment on and off campus included such cheap amusements as square dances, chicken suppers, and hikes in the mountains.

During World War II, the federal government requested institutions of higher education to remain open all months of the year in order to meet a growing demand for trained men (and even women) and the operation of the Selective Service Law (NGC, 1943). NGC complied and operated on a full four-quarter schedule; also, it continued its trend of offering students more specialized curricula during the 1940s than it did during the 1930s (NGC, 1943). Male and female students could choose a specific curriculum that would prepare them for various A.B. and B.S. programs such as business, education, and agriculture, each of which would be completed at another institution. Course requirements among male and female students were identical with a few exceptions. Aside from male students' military training requirement, NGC required that male students earn credit for two courses in mathematics and three courses in science; in contrast, women enrolled in physical education courses and were required to earn credit for just one course in mathematics but four courses in science (NGC, 1943). Women also had the option to enroll in a one-year secretarial course or a one- or two-year pre-nursing curriculum (NGC, 1943).

After World War II, the NGC student body grew as young servicemen and veterans took advantage of GI Bill educational benefits. In 1946, NGC was reinstated as a four-year college. NGC assumed a decidedly more conservative identity during the late 1940s and 1950s, a time defined by the Cold War internationally and the civil rights movement and mass resistance regionally and domestically. Emblematic of this swing to the right, the 1955 edition of the university's yearbook, *Cyclops*, prominently featured the military, both of the present and past. Relative to the latter, the *Cyclops* displayed the Confederate bars and stars on its front cover, while its frontispiece showcased one of the many popular paintings capturing General Robert E. Lee's surrender to Ulysses S. Grant at Appomattox Court House in April 1865. Similarly, it subtly emphasized gendered differences, as women students were celebrated for their participation in campus beauty pageants, their designation as the "battalion sweetheart," or their "quiet" and "cheerful" demeanors or "big smiles."

In spite of this more conservative climate, female students embraced a diverse array of curricular and extracurricular pursuits during the 1950s. Specific to the former, more women earned degrees in such female-dominated fields as secretarial science, elementary education, and home economics, but others chose such majors as chemistry, English, or mathematics. Specific to extracurricular pursuits, the number of academic honor societies; professional clubs; athletic teams; and, particularly, religious organizations offered at NGC exploded during the early post-war era, and women were especially well represented in them (Cyclops, 1955). For example, women served on the staff of the *Bugler*, the college's quarterly literary magazine; dominated the Future Teachers of America club; were active in the Baptist Student Union and the Wesley Foundation; and even joined such stereotypically male organizations as the chemistry club and physics club (Cyclops, 1958). Further, NGC established a women's varsity rifle team, fittingly appropriate for the decidedly martial environment of the 1950s (Cyclops, 1958).

The Baby Boom generated a larger-than-ever population of college-ready students, beginning in the mid-1960s and continuing into the early 1980s. Gainesville Junior College (later Gainesville State College) opened its doors in the fall of 1966 and immediately witnessed the emergence of a left-leaning, anti-Vietnam War culture in which women made significant contributions. NGC, in contrast, remained a socially and politically conservative institution during the 1960s. However, change, particularly demographic change, was soon in store for NGC. Nationwide, public support for the military declined in wake of the painful defeat in the Vietnam War. This trend even affected NGC—an institution largely defined by the military training it provided—with a palpable decline of emphasis on the military department. However, this decline of emphasis engendered greater interest in the institution among women. Between 1965 and 1975, the percentage of women students enrolled at NGC catapulted from 25% to 53% (Cyclops, 1975, p. 154). Now in the majority, female students participated in an even wider variety of extracurricular activities and assumed leadership positions on campus. Relative to the latter, in 1975, women filled the positions of vice president, treasurer, and secretary in the NGC student government as well as served as editor of *Cyclops* (1975). Women further embraced their political agency via participation in the Women's Student Government Association, a self-governing organization through which women students actively influenced the broader student government. Two national sororities, Delta Zeta and Phi Mu, established at NGC in 1973 augmented social opportunities for female students. In the almost 50 years since, three other national sororities—Alpha Gamma Delta, Sigma Kappa, and Delta Phi Epsilon—have set up chapters (UNG, n.d.-c).

In 1973, North Georgia College became the first school in the nation to accept women into the Army Reserve Officers' Training Corps (ROTC) (UNG, n.d.-d). However, such women—known on campus as "cadettes"— were segregated from men, donned uniforms different from those worn by men, and drilled only one day per week separately from men. Few women participated in the cadettes (NGC, 1973). The largest number of women enrolled in ROTC at NGC between 1973 and 1977 stood at a mere 18 students; this equated to no more than 4% of the female student body. By the spring of 1977, only two women had been commissioned as officers (Alexander, 1977).

In 1977, women were fully integrated into the Corps of Cadets. In practical terms, this meant that such women would follow the same military routine—including arising at six each morning, dressing in uniform every day, and drilling every day—though female cadets did not barrack with men, drill alongside men, or endure the same physical training (Alexander, 1977). NGC was the third institution—after Texas A&M and Norwich Military Academy—in the country to offer identical military opportunities to its male and female ROTC students. NGC President John Owen, who also served as secretary of the Army's advisory panel on Army ROTC, fully supported the integration. According to Owen, "military training is a wonderful opportunity for women as well as men. The Air Force has always included women, and it's about time the Army did" (Alexander, 1977). Recently, UNG celebrated its first female cadet to achieve the rank of colonel, Greta Railsback, who graduated in 1999 (UNG, 2021b).

Since 1980, NGC has evolved from a military and liberal arts college to a multifaceted university with a more diverse student body and curricular offerings. In 1990, the NGC student population hovered around 2000. The state designated North Georgia College as a university six years later, at which time it morphed into North Georgia College & State University (NGCSU). Since consolidation of NGCSU and Gainesville State College in 2012, the University of North Georgia has witnessed increased interest among women. The latest figures reveal that women comprise nearly 60% of the student body (UNG, 2021a). Also, women continue to distinguish themselves in the Corps of Cadets. Two female students have assumed the highest-ranking position within the Corps of Cadets: the Cadet Brigade Commander. Most recently, Cadet Col. Logan Scott served as Cadet Brigade Commander during the 2019–2020 academic year (Podo, 2019).

Faculty

North Georgia Agricultural College (NGAC) may be exceptional for admitting women students from the day the institution opened its doors in 1873, but equally exceptional is its employing female faculty also from the very beginning. During the institution's inaugural year, eight faculty taught at NGAC, two of whom were women who also happened to be the daughters of President David W. Lewis (NGAC, 1874). Miss Mattie Whitten Lewis served as an assistant in the primary (pre-collegiate) department, while Miss Fannie Grattan Lewis is listed as an instructress of instrumental music (NGAC, 1874). The Lewis daughters did not remain employed at NGAC for long; however, between the mid-1870s and early 1890s, there was often one woman on the faculty, typically as an assistant in the primary department. By the mid-1890s, the NGAC curriculum expanded, and women taught coursework, including elocution, music, English literature, and art, while also serving in more informal roles as advisors and club sponsors.

Well into the 20th century, women continued to represent just a fraction of the faculty. For example, in 1922, just three of the 21 faculty members were female; one held the title of assistant professor of business science, one was an instructor of domestic science, and the third served as the institution's librarian (North Georgia College, 1922). During the 1930s and early 1940s, when NGC operated as a junior college, the total number of faculty had retrenched from its pre-Great Depression highs, and women still typically comprised just over 10% of the faculty. However, NGC experienced a great transformation in the decade following World War II. The number of faculty catapulted to 46 by the 1955–1956 academic year; among those were 10 women, most of whom held advanced degrees and taught a wider variety of subjects than did their pre-World War II counterparts (NGC, 1955). Outside of the classroom, these female faculty commonly assumed the role of advisor to such student organizations as the *Cyclops*, Future Teachers of America, the Home Economics Club, and many others; or they might operate in such complementary roles as pianist to the Glee Club. NGC also expanded its number of auxiliary positions— for example, secretaries, dieticians, bookstore employees, and canteen assistants—and women were very well represented in those ranks.

The 1960s and 1970s witnessed the women's rights movement; a significant component of that movement's aims was expanding women's educational and professional opportunities. Just as the percentage of female students grew dramatically during these years so also did the number of female faculty, albeit at a slower pace. For example, during the 1976–1977 academic year, NGC included 103 faculty, 27 of whom were women (NGC, 1976). These women faculty tended to fill positions in such traditionally female disciplines as education, home economics, social work, and nursing. However, of those 27 female faculty, 20 had been hired since 1970 (NGC, 1976). This growth strongly suggests that NGC consciously sought to address the historical gender disparity in higher education. In the coming years, NGC continued to recruit faculty who better represented the nation's overall gender demographics.

The 1990s saw an emergence of women-led and focused initiatives for faculty and staff. Commencing in 1995, the Women and Leadership

Conference brought women faculty, military members, and community members together to strategize leading within male-dominated institutions through networking, skill-building, and mentoring (NGCSU Digest, 2003). The transition of more female faculty at NGC once again coincided with the growing increase of the female student population. Further, the beginning of notable leadership roles for women in the institutions began to flourish. Gainesville State College's third president and first female president, Martha T. Nesbitt, led in this role from 1997 to 2012, and, as she wrote in her first president's announcement in the *Laker Log* (1997), she sought to work with all faculty and staff "to be the learning place of Northeast Georgia." Under Nesbitt's leadership, the institution saw enrollment triple within a decade, leading to the creation of the Oconee Campus due to this population growth—as well as to Nesbitt's anticipating the need for two-year colleges in Georgia—and earned the recognition of being the first college in Georgia and one of the first in the country to become tobacco-free (Millsap, 2011).

In the 2020s, women comprise almost 53% of the UNG faculty (approximately 1,133 females to 915 male instructors). In 2019, of the faculty classifications of lecturers, assistant professors, associate professors, and full professors, the largest groups were female assistant professors (123), male assistant professors (114), and female lecturers (106) (UNG employs 237 assistant professors, 141 associate professors, and 171 lecturers) (UNG, 2021a). While women make up more of the academic instructors, in the higher-ranking positions, men continue to be more prevalent in the positions of associate professor and full professor, suggesting efforts still need to be made to address the leaky pipeline. This need is surprising for an institution that, as of 2022, has four of its seven dean positions held by women. One hundred percent of the nursing faculty are women, with the nursing program being one of the largest degree granters for women at UNG (UNG, n.d.-b). However, one of the largest degree producers of male graduates, the Mike Cottrell College of Business, is led by a female dean, and its two associate deans are female; it also has a higher-than-national average of women faculty within their program (UNG, n.d.-a). As we'll read in Chapter 15 (Turner & Jacobs, 2023), during the sesquicentennial celebration, Bonita Jacobs will be celebrating her 12th year as the university's president and as the first female president of NGCSU and through the consolidation into the formation of UNG.

Women's Leadership Organizations

Women of UNG have continuously sought to collectively collaborate toward leadership and fellowship. The evolution of women's organizations throughout the years created seminal events and opportunities for fellowship that would last for decades. Starting in 1966, the Gainesville State College Women's Organization (GSCWO) initiated as an opportunity for female staff, faculty, and spouses of male faculty to congregate to celebrate holidays and end of terms (NGC Digest, 1993). Off-campus luncheons permitted all women of GSU to converse, and the original function of the group was to be a "hostess type group to coordinate college events" (Johnson, 1988). In 1982, GSCWO (renamed Gainesville College Women's Organization [GCWO] in October 1988) sought to create more meaningful engagement, so its first on-campus lunch event included a charitable community component benefitting a local women's domestic violence shelter, the Gateway House (NGC Digest, 1993). Various fundraising activities were complemented over the years to benefit the Gateway House, including yard sales, car shows, silver service donations, and a holiday sing; however, the annual holiday luncheon and auction was the main fundraiser and event of the organization (GCWO).

Comprising a formal board holding monthly meetings and requiring annual dues of $5, the purpose of the GCWO was to "foster social interest among members and support the functions of GSC as an educational, social, and cultural influence in the community" (GCWO Bylaws, 1988). While initially composed as a social organization, additional philanthropy undertakings redirected the organization to the commitment of "more service than social," which led to the creation of student book scholarships, Salvation Army volunteer service, and activities supporting the campus (GCWO Bylaws, 1994). Continuing to contribute to the group's fundraising efforts as well as its focus on supporting women, in 2001, GCWO created the Diana C. Carpenter Memorial Scholarship, in memory of a beloved staff member who had died from cancer, to benefit a non-traditional female student (Kiser, personal communication, April 15, 2022). At the same time, GCWO decided to increase fundraising efforts and awareness of the Gateway House (as well as a second women's charity, Project Safe) by opening up the annual holiday luncheon to all staff and faculty, regardless of gender.

Its last formal luncheon was held by the GCWO in 2012 and was themed Blue Christmas and served roasted goose in honor of the GSC's mascot, Laker T. Goose. GCWO was dissolved in February 2013 as no longer a sanctioned event under consolidation (Kiser, personal communication, April 15, 2022). However, in what UNG now knows as Helpful Harvest, UNG Staff Counsel revived and reinstated the annual auction and fundraising lunch in 2014 to benefit the university's campus food pantry and student scholarships. Kristie Kiser, GCWO president from 2012 to 2013, noted that as of 2021, the annual holiday luncheon represents "the 56th time that women intentionally gathered on the Gainesville campus to bring holiday cheer to their community" (personal communication, April 15, 2022).

Today, UNG continues to create spaces for the fellowship and development of women. The Women's Leadership Initiative (est. 2015) hosts financial planning series, ethical workshops, empowering events, and has established a mentoring program, while the Women of UNG connect and collaborate with alumnae (AccessWDUN, 2016). UNG faculty member Dr. Rosaria Meek, 2021 president of Georgia Association of Women in Higher Education, invited all women of UNG to engage in the association as a means of "cultivating a culture of care and advancement for women in higher education" (Georgia Association, 2022). MSA hosts multiple events and awards to highlight and support the impacts the women of UNG have had on our university and beyond. Through multiple transitions and decades, women at UNG have traversed many firsts to create a place where women can learn, grow, collaborate, and lead.

References

AccessWDUN (2016, March 20). University of North Georgia celebrates Women's History Month with Women's Leadership Initiative. Retrieved April 14, 2022, from https://accesswdun.com/

article/2016/3/378732/university-of-north-georgia-celebrates-
womens-history-month-with-the-womens-leadership-initiative

Alexander, R. (1977, April 8). This is the army, miss jones: North Georgia
integrates women into Cadet Corps. *Atlanta Constitution.*

Boney, F. N. (2000). *A pictorial history of The University of Georgia.*
University of Georgia Press.

Fincher, C. (2005). University System of Georgia. *New Georgia
Encyclopedia.* Retrieved May 18, 2022, from https://www.
georgiaencyclopedia.org/articles/education/university-system-of-
georgia/

Gainesville College Women's Organization (1988, 1994). Bylaws.
University of North Georgia Library.

Georgia Association for Women in Higher Education (2022). Retrieved
April 14, 2022, from https://gawhe.wpcomstaging.com

Johnson, R. (1988, October 14). *Hearts of gold.* The Times: Gainesville.
University of North Georgia Library.

Mewborn, D. S. (2004). Public education. *New Georgia Encyclopedia.*
Retrieved May 18, 2022, from https://www.georgiaencyclopedia.org/
articles/education/public-education-prek-12/

Millsap, J. (2011, August 8). *Gainesville State College president Martha
Nesbitt announces plans to retire effective June 30, 2012.* University
System of Georgia Communications.

Nesbitt, M. T. (1997, April 4). *Laker Log: Gainesville College. 15*(24).
University of North Georgia Library.

North Georgia Agricultural College (1874). *Bulletin.*

North Georgia Agricultural College (1879). *Bulletin.*

North Georgia Agricultural College (1891). *Bulletin.*

North Georgia Agricultural College (1898). *Bulletin.*

North Georgia Agricultural College (1915). *Cyclops* [Yearbook]. University
of North Georgia Library.

North Georgia College (1922). *Bulletin.*

North Georgia College (1931). *Bulletin.*

North Georgia College (1943). *Bulletin.*

North Georgia College (1955). *Bulletin.*

North Georgia College (1973). *Bulletin.*

North Georgia College (1976). *Bulletin.*

North Georgia College (1945). *Cyclops* [Yearbook]. University of North Georgia Library.

North Georgia College (1955). *Cyclops* [Yearbook]. University of North Georgia Library.

North Georgia College (1958). *Cyclops* [Yearbook]. University of North Georgia Library.

North Georgia College (1965). *Cyclops* [Yearbook]. University of North Georgia Library.

North Georgia College (1975). *Cyclops* [Yearbook]. University of North Georgia Library.

North Georgia College Digest (1993, February 15). Profile: The family of North Georgia College.

North Georgia College and State University Digest (2003, March, 3). Women & Leadership Conference planned for March 4. *11*(13).

Podo, K. (2019, August 23) UNG brigade commander encourages women to 'get out there.' *Gainesville Times.*

Roberts, W. P. (1998). *Georgia's best kept secret: A history of North Georgia College.* Alumni Association of North Georgia College.

University of North Georgia (2021a). Common Data Set, 2020–21. [Dashboard] https://ung.edu/institutional-effectiveness/institutional-research/common-data-set.php

University of North Georgia (2021b). *Greta Railsback alumni profile.* https://ung.edu/where-i-lead/alumni/railsback-greta.php

University of North Georgia (n.d-a.). *Mike Cottrell College of Business Faculty.* https://ung.edu/mike-cottrell-college-of-business/faculty-staff.php

University of North Georgia (n.d-b.). *Nursing Department Faculty.* https://ung.edu/nursing/contact.php

University of North Georgia (n.d-c.). *Panhellenic sororities.* https://ung.edu/fraternity-sorority-life/sorority.php

University of North Georgia (n.d-d.). *Women in the Corps of Cadets.* https://ung.edu/military- college-admissions/learn-more/boars-head-brigade/women-in-the-corps.php

Athletics at the University of North Georgia

Walker McCrary and Kelly Britsky

Introduction

Collegiate athletics have long served as a vehicle for various higher education stakeholders—students, alumni, faculty, and staff—to demonstrate pride in their institution, engage the broader community, and even define their individual identities (Clotfelter, 2019; Cohan, 2019; Thelin, 2011). As indicated by other chapters in this volume, which concern the impacts of consolidation, alumni engagement, and community engagement, the University of North Georgia (UNG or North Georgia) is not much different from other institutions in terms of its relationship with athletics (Crowe et al., 2023; Pearl, 2023), but its unique history and traditions are distinctive. Whether through winning championships, graduating student-athletes, or participating in community involvement, athletics has made its mark in all three aspects of the Division II mantra of "Life in the Balance" (NCAA, 2014). UNG's student-athletes have excelled in all three facets of that mantra: comprehensive learning and academic development, high-level athletics competition, and community engagement.

In particular, the athletics department has played a key role in cultivating campus culture throughout the years. Games have always served as a coming together of students, fans, and community. From Spirit Night pep rallies that combine dance teams, live DJs, and food festivals to celebrate various sports events to homecoming weekends that attract UNG graduates from throughout the country, the campus rallies around UNG's nearly 250 student-athletes every time they take the playing field. The university spirit surrounding athletics dates back to the early days of North Georgia, when all student-athletes were cadets and the members of the corps would support their fellow companions in the "battles" that transpired on various courts, tracks, and fields. This chapter is intended to honor the history of UNG's athletic programs while providing a glimpse into the traditions and cultures that have endured the institution's many transitional phases.

The Early History of North Georgia Athletics

Upon the institution's founding in 1873, athletics immediately became an integral part of student life on campus. Inaugural students to the institution could participate in football, basketball, and cross country. However, due to the economic damage on higher education incurred during the Great Depression of the 1930s (Schrecker, 2009) as well as national debates about player injuries and deaths (Carvalho & Baker, 2019), football was dropped. After North Georgia College became a four-year institution in 1949, it joined the Georgia Intercollegiate Athletic Conference (GIAC), a group of eight similarly sized private and public institutions that included Berry College, LaGrange College, Oglethorpe University, Piedmont College, Shorter College, Valdosta State College, and West Georgia College (Thaxton, 1958). The "Cadets" and "Rangers" competed in basketball, tennis, and baseball until the athletic program was disbanded in 1960 due to funding issues.

When John Owen became president of North Georgia College in 1970, he asked the University of Georgia to evaluate the feasibility of restarting the athletics department. This move ignited the spirit and culture still seen at today's athletic events. Harbin "Red" Lawson, the head men's basketball coach at UGA, recommended hiring one of his former "Bulldogs," Bill Ensley, as the men's basketball coach and athletic director of the revitalized program in Dahlonega. In 1971, the "Saints," with a mascot of a Saint Bernard, took the court for the first time. Coach Ensley was critical to the growth and success of the athletic program as he served as athletic director for the next 24 years. He also held the reigns of the men's basketball program for 18 years. Coach Ensley's impact was recognized in 2010, when he was inducted into the North Georgia Athletics Hall of Fame, and in 2015, when the court inside Memorial Hall was renamed in his honor.

The NAIA Era

From 1971 to 2014, North Georgia men's athletics teams battled as a member of the GIAC in the National Association of Intercollegiate Athletics (NAIA). At the outset of this NAIA era, the Saints fielded teams in baseball, men's basketball, and men's tennis. One year later, in 1972, women's basketball, women's volleyball, and men's soccer were added. The Saints were known for their competitive and intimidating crowds that filled Memorial Hall and facilities across campus. A conference basketball game could become an opponent's nightmare on Corps Night, when platoons of cadets filled the gym wearing their colors. At night, the crowds made it difficult to hear coaches or even the officials' whistles.

The women's basketball team played in the Association of Intercollegiate Athletics for Women until 1981, when they also joined the GIAC. One of the highlights, if not *the* highlight, of the NAIA era was the 1986–1987 women's basketball team. Under the direction of head coach Lynne Jarrett, the Saints started off the year with 14 straight wins before dropping two in a row at the midpoint of the season. The community nevertheless rallied around the women's basketball team as they made a run at the NAIA National Championship by winning nine out of the final 10 games of the regular season. After securing the regional title with a 111-100 win over Francis Marion, the Saints traveled to Kansas City, Missouri, for the national championship tournament of 16 women's basketball teams. During the tournament, North Georgia played four games in five days, starting with an opening round 86-70 win over Indiana University-Purdue University Indianapolis (IUPUI). A day later, North Georgia tallied a dominant 82-51 win over Wingate in the national quarterfinals. A win over Wisconsin-Green Bay in the semifinals by a score of 85-76 set up the school's first ever national championship appearance against Southwestern Oklahoma. In heartbreaking fashion, the Bulldogs from Southwestern Oklahoma scored a late shot to narrowly win the national title by a score of 60-58, ending the unprecedented run by the North Georgia Saints.

Although both volleyball and baseball were discontinued during the mid-1980s, women's softball was established as a new sport at North Georgia. The softball program began as a slow-pitch program converting to fast-pitch in 1997. From 1996 to 2000, the athletic program continued to grow as men's and women's cross country and women's soccer were included, and baseball made a triumphant return to campus. Under the direction of legendary Coach Todd Cantrell, the baseball team qualified for six straight NAIA Region tournaments, winning the regional championship in 2002 and 2004. Hall of Famer Bill Ensley's men's basketball teams captured six conference championships, secured bids to five regional tournaments, and played in two NAIA national tournaments. During the 1995–1996 season, UNG Athletics Hall of Fame Coach Randy Dunn's men's basketball team captured both a regular-season championship and a conference tournament championship en route to the NAIA National Tournament. Women's soccer, only two years after its inception, captured back-to-back conference championships in 2000 and 2001 under the leadership of Coach Curly Denier. Softball also got off to a fast start as Coach Ricky Sanders's group qualified for the NAIA Region Tournament twice and won a conference tournament in 2000, just three years into the program's notable history. Coach Mike Davenport led the final years of North Georgia's NAIA era in softball with three conference championships and two trips to the NAIA National Tournament, finishing in the Elite Eight in 2005.

The NCAA Division II Era

With NAIA success under its belt and changes in conference alignment occurring throughout the state, North Georgia transitioned to Division II of the National Collegiate Athletic Association (NCAA) during the 2004–2005 academic year. During that season, North Georgia also joined the Peach Belt Conference. As of this book's publication, the Peach Belt Conference consists of 11 full member institutions in Florida, Georgia, and South Carolina. Many of the institutions—such as Augusta University, Clayton State University, Columbus State University, Georgia College and State University, and Georgia Southwestern State University—are members of the University System of Georgia. Others are either private institutions (such as Flagler College, Lander University, and Young Harris College) or public universities in another state (such as the University of South Carolina-Aiken and University of South Carolina-Beaufort).

Although North Georgia was compelled to serve a three-year probationary period as a new member of the NCAA, the Saints took full advantage of their membership in the NCAA during the 2007–2008 season as both baseball and softball immediately dominated their respective diamonds and earned berths to the NCAA regional tournaments. Since entering the NCAA era, Coach Davenport's softball teams have been particularly successful, winning 11 championships in the Peach Belt Conference and earning invitations to every annual NCAA tournament. The 2015 season was magical, as the UNG softball team brought gold from Oklahoma City to Dahlonega. UNG entered the eight-team tournament as one of the favorites to bring home the hardware but was initially dealt a tough blow by a strong Indianapolis team, which delivered an opening round no-hit game. UNG also went without a hit during the initial three innings of their first elimination game against St. Mary's of Texas, but senior Tiffanie Burns snapped the drought with a solo homer in the fourth, and Meagan May delivered with a walk-off double in the bottom of the eighth to keep UNG alive in the tournament. The softball team was dominant during their next three games, sending home Adelphi with an 8-0 win, and beating Shorter College, their old NAIA foe, twice in the semifinals. UNG faced Dixie State University from St. George, Utah, in the winner-take-all national championship game. The softball team used a four-run second inning and a two-hit shutout from National Player of the Year Courtney Poole to secure the university's first ever national title.

North Georgia athletics went through a period of transition in 2013 when the University System of Georgia consolidated several state institutions. As noted in other chapters, North Georgia College & State University was consolidated with Gainesville State College to become what is now known as the University of North Georgia. The institution reached out to the student body to select a new mascot representing the growing institution. After a student body vote in October 2012, 51% of UNG's students chose the Nighthawk as their new mascot, heavily favored over the other finalists: Golden Eagles and Warriors. Today, students often rub the beaks of Nighthawk statues on each of the five UNG campuses for good luck on upcoming athletic events or exams.

Nevertheless, UNG athletics has needed little luck for Peach Belt Conference success through awards and championships. Since 2012, men's tennis has had eight trips to postseason tournaments. Women's cross country took home the Peach Belt championship hardware in 2017, and the nationally acclaimed rifle program has dominated since 2013–2014, winning seven Georgia State Championships and five Senior Military College Championships. The team sent its first representative to the national championship in 2021–2022, as Kimberlee Nettles qualified in the air rifle discipline.

Under Coach Buffie Burson's direction, women's basketball surged onto the scene in 2018 with a Peach Belt Conference Championship. Since 2018, they have had four conference championships and five NCAA regional berths, including an Elite Eight appearance in 2019 and a historic run to the national semifinals in 2022. Julianne Sutton was also named WBCA National Player of the Year in 2022, following in the footsteps of Hall of Famer Jaymee Carnes, who received Division II National Player of the Year honors after leading the nation in scoring at 25 points per game in 2011–2012. In 2021—the fifth year of the track and field program's existence—UNG earned its second national title as Journey Gurley won the Division II pole vault national championship with a record height of 4.25 meters.

In the Classroom

For any athletic department, winning on the field is important. However, UNG also prides itself on the academic standards that have been established over the past 150 years. The athletic department consistently devotes time and resources to the comprehensive development of its student-athletes; they not only take pride in wins but also celebrate and emphasize character development, sportsmanship, and academic success. UNG student-athletes have been up for the challenge throughout the university's history, but since joining the NCAA, the program has been increasingly honored for its academic excellence.

Season after season, North Georgia's student-athletes have raised the cumulative grade point average of the department, culminating in a record

3.30 cumulative GPA during the 2020–2021 academic year. Each year, the Peach Belt Conference asks each of its members to submit an average GPA for all undergraduates and for the student-athletes; these statistics are then calculated to determine which institution's student-athletes are performing most ahead of the curve in comparison to the student body as a whole. Starting in the 2016–2017 academic year, UNG has consistently won the Peach Belt Conference's President's Academic Award recognizing excellence in academics.

In the Community

In addition to the successes on the playing fields and in the classroom, North Georgia has gone above and beyond to support the community, both locally and nationally. For example, UNG continues to be the leader in fundraising for the *Make-A-Wish Foundation*. To date, UNG's student-athletes have raised over $200,000, granting over 20 wishes to children with life-threatening illnesses. North Georgia has hosted 11 Make-A-Wish kids on campus over the past decade as part of the initiative; it has also won the LeeAnn Noble Make-A-Wish Award for most funds raised in the Peach Belt Conference for each of the past 12 years.

A source of pride for UNG is its identity as one of six federally designated military colleges in the nation. As a reflection of that important designation, the athletic department proudly participates in the Operation Nighthawks of Honor initiative, recognizing service members who were former or are current students. Athletic teams pay tribute to those service members with a ceremony and donate all proceeds from the initiative to the Boar's Head Brigade Corps of Cadets. Donations from a silent auction of the mementos used throughout the year raise funds for the UNG Corps of Cadets Endowment Fund. Nighthawk Athletics has donated over $3,700 to the endowment fund since the initiative's inception on the 14th anniversary of the September 11 attacks. In 2017, the operation won the NCAA's highest honor when it was awarded the NCAA Award of Excellence, again putting UNG in the national spotlight.

UNG athletics continues to bring alumni together through the Nighthawks Athletic Club and the Athletics Hall of Fame. As part of Alumni

Weekend, the Nighthawks Athletic Club—of which many members are university alumni—has annually organized a scholarship golf tournament for the past 47 years. The Athletics Hall of Fame, established in 2010, has inducted 11 classes of former student-athletes, staff, donors, and teams, including former athletes and coaches from years before the NAIA era.

Nighthawk athletes, coaches, and staff are deeply involved with their communities, individually and collectively. Their activities support UNG's mission to develop not only model student-athletes but also socially responsible citizens. The NCAA Division II philosophy statement emphasizes the holistic development of students, as well as community engagement (NCAA, 2013). UNG embraces those beliefs and knows community experiences contribute to the development of leadership and respect.

Conclusion

The rich history of UNG athletics has been cultivated from dedication, hard work, and sweat. UNG student-athletes, coaches, and supporters have long reflected the institution's mission and vision of leadership, integrity, and service while teaching leadership, loyalty, and teamwork. College athletics at UNG directly reflects the heartbeat of the university itself.

Athletics at UNG also continues to play a significant role in the culture and pride of the institution. Although the two national championships and nearly 100 conference championships over the past 50 years are vividly remembered, the legacy of the thousands of student-athletes who have represented their university with honor and unyielding effort are also worthy of celebration. The coaches and students of UNG have continuously worked toward one common goal: to build and maintain highly competitive intercollegiate programs that rank among the elite in both the Peach Belt Conference and in NCAA Division II athletics.

References

Clotfelter, C. T. (2019). *Big-time sports in American universities* (2nd ed.). Cambridge University Press.

Cohan, N. (2019). *We average unbeautiful watchers: Fan narratives and the reading of American sports.* University of Nebraska Press.

National Collegiate Athletics Association (NCAA). (2013). Division II philosophy statement. https://www.ncaa.org/sports/2013/11/15/division-ii-philosophy-statement.aspx

National Collegiate Athletics Association (NCAA). (2014). Life in the balance. https://www.ncaa.org/sports/2014/9/25/life-in-the-balance.aspx

Schrecker, E. (2009, June 16). The bad old days: How higher education fared during the Great Depression. *Chronicle of Higher Education.* https://www.chronicle.com/article/the-bad-old-days/

Thaxton, J. R. (1958). President's annual report, 1957-1958. https://vtext.valdosta.edu/xmlui/handle/10428/1095

Thelin, J. (2011). *A history of American higher education* (2nd ed.). Johns Hopkins University Press.

THERE ARE NO COINCIDENCES: THE LEADERSHIP AND LEGACIES OF LT. COL. CHANDLER R. BROWN JR. AND COL. BEN PURCELL

Anna C. Brown

The University of North Georgia (UNG) is designated as one of six senior military colleges and has a long history of preparing men and women for military service. W. P. Roberts (1998) notes that UNG supported military training from its early days as North Georgia Agricultural College (NGAC). During World War I, the War Department established a training unit at the college that resulted in some of the highest enrollment numbers the institution had experienced in its early decades. The rich tradition of the Corps of Cadets was amplified in 1946 when the Board of Regents "announced its intention to reconvert North Georgia College into a four-year, degree-granting institution" (Roberts, 1998, p. 45). President of the College from 1933 to 1949, Jonathan Clark Rogers oversaw the conversion of the two-year institution to the four-year senior military institution and worked to seek the funding needed to support the expansion of institutional offerings. In the 1960s, the Corps of Cadets program was viewed as highly successful due to outstanding ratings from visiting inspectors as well as top scores from cadets at summer camp competitions (Roberts, 1998). The performances of outstanding cadets, top-ranking military officers, and highly decorated military alumni continue to be realized by members of the UNG community. The importance of the military tradition to the institution started in the early years of its founding. UNG remains committed to producing officers who will serve the nation through their leadership, and some leaders have built a lasting legacy through their service in guiding the next generation of cadets.

Legacy and *leadership* are terms that are interwoven outcomes of a story that began in the 1960s and persist today due to the chance meeting of two men at a small military junior college in Missouri. In fact, if it were not for their encounter, I would not be here to write the story you are about to read. My father is Retired Lieutenant Colonel Chandler Russell Brown Jr., and he has a deep connection to the University of North Georgia that spans over 50 years. In early September 2021, Lt. Col. Brown took the time to tell me how he found his way to UNG and the impact of one man's recommendation.

Brown's Story

Early Life

As Lt. Col. Brown describes his childhood and early years with his family, he does not overlook the influence of service and military experience. Brown was the eldest of three siblings from Lowell, Massachusetts, but the family did not stay there. They moved to Germany when he was a young child and continued the pattern of moving to new cities and states throughout his childhood. His father, Col. Chandler R. Brown Sr., was a World War II fighter pilot. Col. Brown Sr. was one of 100 pilots from his flight school class at the start of World War II and one of eight still alive following the war. He was the first Air Force officer to go through helicopter training at Fort Rucker, Alabama, and served as a meteorologist who prepared the weather stations in Thailand, Laos, and Vietnam ahead of the Vietnam War. The full military career of Brown's father required many moves for the family, and Brown attended four different high schools. One of the final moves during Brown's high school years stationed the family at Scott Air Force Base in Bellville, Illinois. Bellville is a two-and-a-half-hour drive from Booneville, Missouri, where Brown would spend his freshmen and sophomore years at Kemper Military School & College.

As Brown's time at the two-year institution was ending, he was trying to decide where to go to complete his four-year degree. The Professor of Military Science for Kemper was Lt. Col. Benjamin H. Purcell, who was a 1950s graduate from North Georgia College in Dahlonega, Georgia. Brown stated that Lt. Col. Purcell "recommended North Georgia College to me and encouraged me to consider going there." After Brown graduated with his Associate of Arts degree from Kemper, he began to research the mountain town of Dahlonega, Georgia, and North Georgia College.

North Georgia College

North Georgia College (NGC) was the next place that Brown went to continue his education. Considering all the praise he had heard from Purcell at Kemper and the opportunity to attend a coed military college, Brown recalled, "At the time I attended, women were not yet allowed in the corps, but they were attending the institution." He admitted that the hope of meeting someone special was an influencing factor. Brown would meet his future wife, Linda Anderson, at the freshman dance at the start of his junior year in 1967. They were both from military families, and each knew someone who had attended NGC and encouraged them to enroll. Brown recalled that "we were both transfer students to NGC and in our junior years, but they still let everyone come to the freshmen dance. It was held right in front of Memorial Hall Gym." Brown would discover later that Linda had an uncle named Sherman Dixon who attended NGC and was a bomber pilot in WWII. Unfortunately, Dixon had been killed in action during the war. His name was engraved on the monument outside of the Memorial Hall Gym where Brown and Linda first met.

Brown studied physical education at NGC and was a member of the Corps of Cadets serving in Bravo company his junior year and as Brigade S-2 his senior year. Brown played as many sports as he could while attending NGC, but his favorite was football. He stated, "In my time, each company had its own football team, and we played in full padding on what is now the promenade outside of the library." In addition to playing football as a member of the corps, he served as vice president of the Officer's Club and treasurer of the Physical Education Club. He also was a member of the Sigma Theta fraternity and the college baseball team.

In June of 1969, Brown graduated from NGC as a Distinguished Military Graduate and received a Regular Army commission. His commissioning ceremony was very meaningful as he recalled "the college let my dad swear me in, and it made for a moment in my life that I will never forget and that I know meant a great deal to my father." Brown and Linda Anderson graduated in the afternoon following his commissioning, and they were married that evening. June 1, 1969, is affectionately noted by their families as the Trifecta: commissioning, graduation, and wedding.

Figure 4.1: LTC Brown received the Distinguished Military Graduate distinction on the drill field.

Brown recalled the important relationships he made and the leaders he encountered during his time at NGC. The top of the list is his wife, Linda, who has shared a life with him for nearly 53 years. He also made close friends with Bill Turman and his wife, Dixie; Turman served in the same brigade with him in Germany. The Browns and Turmans have remained close friends for over 50 years. They recently celebrated their 50th class reunion at UNG in 2019.

One of the leaders who influenced and shaped the officer and man Brown became was Coach Matherly. Matherly was his professor of physical education and his major advisor. Through Matherly's academic support, Brown achieved the grades to earn his bachelor's degree. Another impactful leader mentioned by Brown was Major Tucker, who had recently returned from Vietnam and was serving as a military science professor. Brown was impressed by Tucker's leadership: "Tucker went on to serve as an aide to General Colin Powell, and I was honored to be able to learn from a man of his caliber." These two professors cultivated his academic pursuits and influenced his leadership skills in the Army, fostering his later interest in teaching.

Figure 4.2: Linda Anderson Brown and LTC Brown in front of Dunlap Hall after the commissioning ceremony.

Another important and familiar leader intersected with Brown's time at NGC. While Brown was in his first year at NGC and was working in the chow hall line, he recognized the familiar face of Col. Purcell. Surprised at seeing the man who had recommended the institution now standing in front of him, Brown went over to speak with Col. Purcell and thank him for the recommendation. The two had not seen each other since Brown had graduated from Kemper the year prior, and they took the time to chat. Purcell told Brown he was on his way to Vietnam and was visiting before deployment. Brown said:

Later, I found out that he was shot down and became a POW for I believe 62 months, with 58 of them in solitary confinement. His wife and children had no idea if he was alive or dead for over five years. Once the peace treaty was signed, he was released. He was the highest-ranking Army officer to be a POW in Vietnam.

In retrospect, this encounter with Col. Purcell, right before his departure to Vietnam, meant a great deal to Brown.

After Graduation

As Col. Purcell faced the extreme difficulties of his time as a prisoner of war in Vietnam, Brown began his years of service to the country. Brown reflected on the qualities of the leaders he had known in college and the education they gave him to hone his skills as a leader and trainer in the Army. While stationed in Germany and Korea, he trained and developed evaluation programs for the brigades he served. When he returned to the United States, Brown attended the Officer Advanced Course and was assigned to be the instructor in the Artillery Missile Training Department in Fort Sill, Oklahoma. Brown's dedication to learning, teaching, and leading placed him on the team working on the Pershing Missile and elevated him to the highest level of top-secret clearance during the time he served in active duty.

After nine years of active duty, Brown resigned his Regular Army commission and became a reserve officer in 1978. He had a passion for education, teaching, and training, so he returned once more to NGC to earn a Master of Education. As Brown worked toward completing his Master's Degree, he was teaching a business communications course for the business department. The original recommendation to attend NGC felt like the right decision for Brown to make again as he pursued his next degree. Brown recalled:

As if everything had come full circle, Col. Purcell was the Commandant of Cadets at this same time. I was happy to be once again intersecting with the man who had influenced me to take the path that had brought me to so much of my life's joys. It was his last assignment prior to his retirement, and I was pleased to share in the community of NGC with him.

Working at the institution with Col. Purcell before his retirement in 1980 (Breazeale, 2013) was another highlight for Brown. As he reflected on the powerful leader who helped shape his life in the late 1960s, Brown began a new journey in his own life and moved his young family to Atlanta. He utilized his teaching degrees to become an effective human resources trainer as he worked for several companies during the 1980s.

Return to Dahlonega

In 1991, Brown returned to his favorite mountain town of Dahlonega with his wife and four children. While in the town that he would call home for the next three decades, Brown started his own training company and conducted training programs for businesses around the state of Georgia as well as other parts of the country. Brown used his education degrees to support his efforts teaching in the Economic Development Department for several of the technical colleges of Georgia. He took his final job back at his alma mater in 2010, when it was North Georgia College & State University. Brown taught speech in the Fine Arts Department until the institution became the University of North Georgia in 2013. He taught his final two years in the Communication, Media, and Journalism Department for UNG until he retired in 2015.

Col. Purcell spent his retirement in Clarkesville, Georgia, a short distance from UNG. Brown and Purcell crossed paths over the decades. Purcell was honored at UNG in 2012—one year before his death—with the dedication of the Colonel Ben Purcell Formation Plaza located near the corps residence halls. The ripple effect of Purcell's influence, leadership, and legacy continues as the generations of UNG cadets file into formation on his namesake's plaza; it continues as well in the lives of countless people he inspired through his service, commitment, and bravery to our country. For Lt. Col. Brown, Purcell's influence shaped his entire life in expected and unexpected ways.

The Last Intersection

In April of 2022, I took Lt. Col. Brown to see Purcell Plaza early on a Sunday morning. As we traversed from the Alumni House to the newer residence halls, Brown reminisced about where he had lived on campus. Once we arrived on the plaza, Brown went directly to the placard and read aloud its information:

> Colonel Ben Purcell Formation Plaza. Dedicated April 21, 2012, in honor of Col Ben Purcell, North Georgia College class of 1950, for his courage, military leadership, service to his country, and dedication to his alma mater.

I asked him to reflect on his connection to the man who had first brought him to UNG. When asked if he thought Purcell knew how important the recommendation to attend UNG was in shaping Brown's life, Brown responded:

> I got to talk to him when he was on his last assignment here at UNG and I was getting my master's degree. I shared with him how much I valued his advice. I also attended his funeral in 2013, and I ran into his daughter and shared his influence on my life with her too. She told me that she was born in Booneville, Missouri, where I had first met her father. He had an impact on my life. I wouldn't have known anything about North Georgia without him. I have a lovely wife and four children because of his recommendation.

I followed up by asking what Col. Purcell taught him about leadership and legacy. As we viewed the drill field from the Purcell Plaza, Brown stated:

> Listening to his leadership in recommending this school to me allowed me to be one of the few who were able to get a Regular Army commission, and that was important to me. Our lives continued to intersect again and again because there are no coincidences. I believe God had a role in our interaction, and he [Purcell] was very well respected as you can

see [gesturing to the plaza], and people listened to what he had to say. I listened to what he had to say.

We continued to discuss the impact that leaders, teachers, and coaches could have on their students' lives and how they could not even realize their influence. Brown had been a student, a cadet, a teaching assistant, and a professor at UNG throughout his decades-long connection to the campus we were visiting. When I asked him to reflect on his time at UNG, he stated:

> The University of North Georgia had a major impact on my life. I have enjoyed the opportunity to participate in many levels of the institution. My rich relationship and pathway to UNG would not have happened if my father had not been in the military and I had not attended the college in Missouri. Because he was and I did, I met Col. Benjamin Purcell, who set me on my path to this wonderful home at UNG. To me, there are no coincidences.

After recounting all of Brown's and Purcell's interactions over the decades, we concluded our time on Purcell Plaza; however, the memories and stories from Brown's years at UNG spilled out over breakfast the next morning. The opportunity to visit the plaza had meant a great deal to Brown, and he was excited to point out other changes to the institution over the years. He mentioned how glad he was that we would be able to celebrate UNG's 150 years and that he was fortunate to be around for over a third of the history of UNG.

Figure 4.3: LTC Brown at Purcell Plaza in 2022.

Fig. 4.4: LTC Brown in his 1969 letterman jacket to reminisce.

Conclusion

Lt. Col. Brown's story about UNG and Col. Purcell demonstrates the connectedness of people to a place, the memories they make, and the decisions that steer their lives. Col. Purcell was an extraordinary leader in the eyes of Brown. His legacy continues not only under the feet of the new generations of cadets that line up on Purcell Plaza but also in the stories that people like Brown share with their friends and family. One of Purcell's fellow cadets, Col. Ed Nix, spoke about him after his death in 2013, stating, "he was not only an outstanding cadet, he was an outstanding officer" (Breazeale, 2013, paragraph 3). Purcell's final assignment as the professor of military science had a lasting impression on another student of UNG. Col. Rich Crotty was a member of the Corps of Cadets and remembers, "He mentored us. He was a professional Army officer" (Breazeale, 2013, paragraph 15). Crotty recalled that Purcell used his own experience as a soldier to emphasize to his students the values of family, faith, and love of country.

Perhaps there are no coincidences when it comes to the intersections Brown experienced with Purcell over the decades, or maybe there is something indefinable about the relationships built and the experiences had by those who choose to attend UNG. Brown believes in his connection to a fellow soldier, teacher, and alumus and the importance of listening to one recommendation.

For 150 years, alumni have been recommending UNG to potential students. UNG has adapted and grown over the decades, but the relationships, foundations, and memories formed throughout its history amongst the members of its community serve as great connection points for the future of UNG. Hopefully, there will always be stories like Brown's and Purcell's to remind us of the importance of leadership and legacy at UNG.

References

Breazeale, G.(2013). *Highest-ranking Army POW in Vietnam dies: Purcell led cadets at University of North Georgia.* Retrieved June 17, 2022, from https://www.gainesvilletimes.com/news/highest-ranking-army-pow-in-vietnam-dies/

Roberts, W. P. (1998). *Georgia's best kept secret: A history of North Georgia College*. William P. Roberts and the Alumni Association of North Georgia College.

Successful Cultural Outcomes from the UNG Consolidation: Information Technology, Libraries, University Relations

Ken Crowe, Timothy Daniels, Anna Gibbs, Steven McLeod, and Amanda Nash

The consolidation that formed the University of North Georgia (UNG) from North Georgia College & State University (NGCSU) and Gainesville State College (GSC) in 2012 has been heralded as one of the more successful unions within the University System of Georgia (USG). Much of this success is due to the diligent work of administrators to develop objectives that provided the recipe for the new consolidated university. Prominent throughout UNG's 2014–2019 five-year strategic plan (University of North Georgia, 2014) was an emphasis on the cultural identity of the university and of each individual campus.

This chapter will recount successful cultural outcomes achieved in three organizations—Information Technology, Libraries, and University Relations—that, in many ways, are complementary. Both Libraries and University Relations depend on a reliable infrastructure maintained by Information Technology. Information Technology supports the systems necessary for these two public-facing entities to interact with university constituents. While technology links these three entities, the lessons learned by each pertaining to organizational culture offer models that other organizations faced with substantive change (like a consolidation) can emulate.

Information Technology

Through the lens of information technology (IT), the changes necessary for combining two higher educational institutions were multifaceted. The three primary elements of change were related to technical, procedural, and personnel issues. Each of these primary elements of change have cultural implications, but the personnel- and procedural-related components were the most significant. If either institution had been asked which changes needed to be made in 2012, each would most likely have answered that nothing needed to change. Nevertheless, change was a necessary growing pain for the new university. Funding needed to be rebalanced, departments had to rethink staffing and structure, work had to be realigned to meet different needs, and new staff were needed to fill new necessary positions. Some IT staff commented on the unique opportunity to decide which methods to adopt or change, while others expressed a wish to have been directed into which of the two institution's ways to move. The technical aspects of consolidation represented a significant amount of work in that every information system and management tool previously used by the institutions needed to be inventoried and evaluated for best fit in the new institution. This winnowing exercise may seem to be a logical process that moves quickly, but the reality is that the process runs head-on into culture when a choice has to be made between how the differing products or processes possessed by the two merging institutions impact operations. Pride in what has been developed or in the "way we work" gets in the way, causing personnel clashes and slowing the process down.

The initial round of technical change required for UNG revolved around the most critical systems. Fortunately, general agreement was accorded on the computer operating systems, general office productivity tools, and the student information system. These agreed-upon systems allowed for some quick wins and for the opportunity to move quickly on some important technologies. However, process and "how we do work" perspectives remained an issue, as the two institutions simply worked differently, and those differences were ingrained in the respective cultures. Tuckman's (1965) developmental sequences of forming, storming, norming, performing, and adjourning were on display throughout the teaming exercises. After the initial consolidation, organizational changes were once again required to align with the proper processes for a larger institution, one that was twice the size of the previous institutions and operating on four campuses. This realignment focused on alignment of function versus location to orient and guide the IT teams in the same direction and into alignment with the UNG strategic plan.

The choice of the proper standards of practice for the new UNG was not a major challenge, but the implementation of these changes—along with their cultural implications—certainly was. DiMaggio and Powell (1983) have contended that for institutionalized change to occur in an organization, the normative, mimetic, and coercive isomorphic forces should be applied. These isomorphic forces were utilized to varying degrees in the UNG consolidation as well as within IT. McLeod (2017) recently concluded that in addition to the isometric forces, executive buy-in and an understanding of the changes were important tactics for institutionalizing change in higher education information technology.

Since selecting the standards of practice, UNG IT has made significant advances in its practices and the maturity of its processes. This standardization has greatly impacted the division of information technology's efficiency and effectiveness, cross-functional work, and alignment of the language related to the division's work. The rating of the customer service provided by IT staff and the availability of the services provided is high. IT staff have become more cohesive and aligned to this new UNG way, but the cultural change is still not fully complete, and there is more work to instill mature and institutionalized practices.

Another set of differences between the institutions was realized in the established processes and reporting. Both institutions followed USG guidelines, but implementation of those guidelines looked very different. Whereas one institution focused on one-to-one communication and ad hoc processes that were people-oriented, the other focused on more widespread communication and formal processes targeted to outcomes. Both foci served each institution and their cultures well, but bringing together the two very different work styles proved challenging. Having to decide which method to implement ultimately led to discontent, frustration, and occasionally turnover in some areas. Others viewed change in processes as an opportunity to continue growth and expand into other beneficial ways of working. Not one way was chosen for the entire university; instead, departments were able to form, storm, and norm on what worked best in their new world. Even heading into a decade after consolidation, we are still tweaking the ways of working. Having grown into a much larger community, IT nevertheless has found ways to enhance processes while also showing care and attention to the people.

A final critical component to success was ensuring that employees felt like they had a voice in decisions being made. Decisions were based on what would be best for the university versus one side or the other "winning" the decision. By allowing the institutions to decide how to move forward, a lot of freedom was allowed in the process. However, the freedom led to serious debate and divisiveness at times. By inviting faculty and staff to meetings to discuss campus strengths and weaknesses, a new UNG culture started to emerge.

Libraries

Before consolidation in 2012, the cultures of the GSC and NGCSU libraries were distinctly different. Their physical facilities, organizational structures, internal processes and procedures, and faculty roles and responsibilities reflected not only a difference in the mission of the institutions and their student demographics but also a sharp divergence in resources and their philosophical approaches to library services.

The Library Technology Center at NGCSU was built in 2008, housing traditional library collections and service points, classroom space, and a coffee shop, along with writing tutors and the IT help desk. This information commons approach reflected the predominant trend in library design at the time, particularly for libraries serving four-year students on residential campuses. The NGCSU library enjoyed staffing levels commensurate with the facility's size and operational needs, consisting of access services and technical services departments as well as a team of reference and instruction librarians. Librarians at NGCSU were non-tenure-track faculty reporting directly to the head of the library, a director-level position. The library faculty at NGCSU operated on a true library liaison model. Each academic department had a librarian assigned to provide library instruction for courses in the discipline and to assist with collection development efforts.

Choosing materials for the collection was, however, driven by teaching-faculty requests; librarians would share book lists and reviews of available materials but did not make any selections directly or independently. The NGCSU librarians taught instructional sessions for courses and workshops but did not teach any credit-bearing courses themselves, although one credit-bearing class was under development.

GSC was already operating as a multi-campus institution before consolidation, and both the Gainesville and Oconee campuses included library facilities. The John Harrison Hosch Library at the Gainesville Campus was built in 1970. At the time of consolidation, the facility solely housed library operations, as media and IT offices had moved out with the opening of the Martha T. Nesbitt Academic Building in 2012. The Oconee Campus library, located in the Student Resource Center building, came with its collections in place when the campus was acquired from Truett-McConnell College in 2003. These older library buildings reflected the size and instructional focus of the campuses when they were built, and the student populations had outgrown the facilities at both locations by the mid-2000s. Staffing was inadequate, along with square footage; as a result, the GSC libraries did not operate with any traditional library departments per se. The librarians at GSC were tenure-track faculty, reporting to a dean of libraries, and had taught face-to-face and online credit-bearing research skills courses for many years. Operationally, GSC libraries practiced a hybrid approach. Collection development activities were undertaken by librarian liaisons who represented each college at each campus (e.g., the College of STEM had a liaison at Gainesville and Oconee). Each campus collection was distinct and separate. Materials were selected by both faculty requests and librarian analysis and identification. Instruction, on the other hand, was divided by campus but not by discipline, with the library faculty at each location providing course-related instruction for any course based upon availability, not subject expertise.

These very different library organizations had undertaken a cooperative partnership in 2012, collaborating on the library presence at the new joint instructional site in Forsyth County, which would become UNG's Cumming Campus. This facility had no physical collection of materials, but the NGCSU and GSC library leaders worked together to make operational decisions, select equipment, and choose finishes for the new facility.

Post-consolidation, the UNG libraries adopted a location-driven organizational structure without any traditional library departmental divisions. The new structure was led by the former GSC dean of libraries, who retained that title, and a head librarian representing each of the four campuses. Staffing at each facility remained the same as preconsolidation; no personnel were relocated among campuses. Library faculty members voted to adopt tenure-track faculty status for all librarians. Functionally, the UNG libraries merged the library catalogs and associated circulation policies and processes. Likewise, collection development took a universal approach, with selection responsibilities divided by disciplines but not by location, with each librarian considering both faculty requests and their own expertise in identifying and choosing materials for all library facilities. Instruction, however, became a location-based activity, with lower-level courses being taught by "all hands," while some specializations evolved for upper-level course instruction.

The one advantage to this location-based approach was that the existing differences at each campus—including facilities, student demographics, and operational histories—were front of mind. The disadvantages, however, were practical and ideological. Maintaining a location-based structure created communication challenges that hampered the smooth operation of basic library functions. With no one directly involved in specific day-to-day operations in charge of running them, and with people at every campus working on these functions without strong coordination, operations either struggled to be tackled globally or remained local in focus. Strides were made in some areas—circulation and processing of materials, in particular—but other areas struggled. In addition, the location-driven approach kept old perspectives and mindsets in place: local thinking prevailed.

The maintenance of a location-driven structure became unsustainable, and with a change in leadership at the dean's level in July 2019, a reorganization was undertaken. This reorganization was intended to create and implement traditional library functional divisions, like Technical Services and Reference and Instruction, populated by library faculty and staff from various campuses based on individual skills, responsibilities, and operational needs. The head librarian position was eliminated, and division-based leadership was put in place, along with a librarian point-person identified at each campus to address facility-related matters. Microsoft Teams served as a vehicle for communication directly between division colleagues and libraries personnel as a whole.

This new structure became effective in January 2020, just before the shift to online operations necessitated by COVID-19. Surprisingly, the adoption of the new structure was facilitated by pandemic operations, as all library personnel were forced to rapidly implement Teams and to focus on service functions, not locations. Further initiatives to aid communication and boost morale during the pandemic helped to begin to shift the culture and create a more cohesive, consolidated library department. During this difficult time, personnel got to know their colleagues at other campuses through online social activities and collaboration to face new challenges. Since the return to campus and shift back to pre-COVID-19 processes, some old patterns, such as reverting to outdated location-based processes and holding operational discussions off of the Teams platform where cross-campus participation could take place, have reemerged, demonstrating the iterative nature of cultural change.

Ideally, a consolidation examines and evaluates existing operations and creates a new unified organizational culture. Changing an organization's culture takes time and understanding. Bolman and Deal (2017) proposed a model for examining organizations that uses four frames (structural, human resource, political, and symbolic) for evaluating an organization to give leaders a diverse perspective for determining the organization's current state and deciding where change needs to happen. Durant (1999) described a three-phase system that includes unfreezing, learning, and refreezing. During the unfreezing stage, the team managing change begins the process of shifting the organizational culture by preparing the staff to learn a new system. In the second phase, learning strategies are developed, new policies and procedures are created, and the team is prepared for a cultural change. In the third stage, refreezing, a new organizational culture is established. Even though library management did not explicitly work through Bolman and Deal's processes of framing—or through Durant's phases of unfreezing, learning, and refreezing—during consolidation, the initial years of operating as consolidated libraries accomplished the process of reframing the libraries as an organization, and cultural change slowly began. The biggest win was that the consolidation of the libraries started an ongoing change process that has provided an opportunity to better serve all UNG's students.

University Relations

Higher education consolidation is a lengthy process that involves the reformation of each institution's cultural identity (Harman, 2002). Organizational culture defines the social fabric of higher education, where practices are rooted in values and traditions (Välimaa, 2008). Institutional change is most effective when strategies are aligned with the organizational culture. Prior to the formation of UNG, NGCSU and GSC had long established their own individual missions, cultures, and traditions. Kate Maine, UNG's Vice President of University Relations and Chief of Staff, served on the consolidation committee that took on the unique task of identifying and incorporating central artifacts from both institutions into the newly consolidated university. Maine shared that, in the early stages of forming UNG, leadership communication increased significantly and campus community and alumni were engaged, establishing a collaborative approach to consolidation. The new name, new mission, new mascot, and new brand were each essential in establishing the new institutional identity of UNG.

In launching the name "University of North Georgia," the implementation planning committee involved various stakeholders in the process through focus groups and surveys. Alumni from NGCSU and GSC were passionate and engaged about the name of the newly formed institution. Both NGCSU and GSC had been through various name changes throughout the years. Although stakeholder input elongated the process of naming the institution, it also greatly increased buy-in for the new name. University President, Bonita Jacobs, stated in a May 2012 press release that the "University of North Georgia is a forward-looking name that creates a strong identity for this new university that spans a large geographic region and that will have such a broad array of educational programs serving a student population of more than 15,000" (as cited in Couret, 2012, para. 3). This name prevailed because it allowed the institution to establish a regional identity. Located in the fastest-growing region in the state, UNG's five campuses span across 30 predominantly rural counties, situated just north of metro Atlanta. Approximately 80% of UNG's student body are located in the 30-county area (UNG, n.d.). The provision of accessible educational opportunities for this region has prompted many alumni to remain in the region, thus benefitting the economic development of the North Georgia region. The establishment of the UNG mission statement involved leveraging each of the legacy institution's strengths. Mission statements act as a guide for a university by articulating a shared sense of purpose and providing a vision for an institution's future. Moreover, a mission statement can inspire and motivate those within an institution while providing information to external constituents (Morphew & Hartley, 2006). NGCSU was rooted in a historic military mission, while GSC was devoted to access. The consolidated mission statement honored both of the legacy institutions' missions. Stakeholder input on the new mission statement was collected through campus-based workshops and focus groups. UNG kept NGCSU's designation as a senior military college and the Military College of Georgia. Simultaneously, UNG maintained GSC's mission of access by expanding throughout the region and maintaining affordability. Consolidation often comes with a fear of losing institutional identity; however, the UNG consolidation exemplifies how a successful consolidation can respect each legacy institution's mission through accumulation of resources and opportunities.

While the name and mission statement were essential for Board of Regents approval and accreditation, the community played an influential role in the development of the UNG mascot. Selection of the mascot was a largely debated issue, as each institution brought their own mascot that served to support student activities and programs. The process of identifying the new mascot began with researching animals indigenous to the North Georgia region and soliciting suggestions from alumni, students, and community members. Ultimately, the finalization of the Nighthawk as the UNG mascot was decided by a student vote. Nigel the

Nighthawk symbolized the inception of UNG and lead to an increase in internal rallying for the unification.

In another attempt to build campus identity and institutional unity at the newly established UNG, the brand platform Lead Where It Counts was developed. The brand was developed to focus on the institution's role as a state leadership institution. Lead Where It Counts highlights many forms of leadership across all campuses, including the Corps of Cadets on the Dahlonega Campus, first-generation college students, and activists within the university community. The brand strives to help students see themselves as leaders and to develop leadership skills needed for future success. The brand also strives to help faculty and staff think about leadership and its many forms. The brand development is an ongoing process that will be built over many years.

Consolidation successes from a university relations perspective are plenty. UNG was designated a top producer of Fulbright Scholars in 2018. Opportunities that have been made possible because of the consolidation include newly generated resources, growth in institutional research, the expansion of academic programs, and a new standalone campus. Evidence of student successes includes enrollment growth across all campuses and increased retention and graduation rates. Each of these successful outcomes has contributed to the amplified reputation of UNG.

Conclusion

Institutional culture is a primary way that stakeholders identify with a higher education institution (Toma et al., 2005). Additionally, institutional culture has been shown to be a chief concern during mergers of higher educational institutions (Azziz et al., 2019). This narrative of the cultural successes of three organizations at the University of North Georgia is an example of how new cultures can be formed during a higher education merger. In looking at the three complementary units of Information Technology, Libraries, and University Relations, similarities of cultural change become evident.

People and infrastructure must work in concert to successfully usher in cultural change. As noted by Information Technology, staff can be married to legacy systems in a way that impedes changes. Libraries noted that initial attempts to serve the new UNG were restricted by physical location and size of facility. For University Relations, the institutional name and mascot changes enabled the new university to be more inclusive.

While infrastructure support elements can provide an avenue toward a new culture, constituent buy-in is essential for success. For the three units portrayed, personnel and organization changes were inevitable. During these changes, the support of senior leaders in the institution was essential to align everyone with the new strategies and encourage buy-in. Throughout the consolidation process, the focus on culture and the solicitation of stakeholder input in establishing the name, mission, mascot, and brand of UNG were instrumental in developing the institution's new identity.

While consolidation is a stressful process that inevitably results in some loss of institutional identity, Maine described how a feeling of unity developed at UNG through an appreciation of cultural differences across each of the five campuses. As we approach the sesquicentennial celebration, we also approach the 10th anniversary of the consolidation. This time provides the opportunity to reflect on not only the past progress and future direction of the University of North Georgia but also how cultural differences can leverage individual strengths to forge an innovative and responsive institution.

References

Azziz, R., Hentschke, G. C., Jacobs, L. A., & Jacobs, B. C. (2019). *Strategic mergers in higher education.* Johns Hopkins University Press.

Bolman, L. G., & Deal, T. E. (2017). *Reframing organizations: Artistry, choice, and leadership* (6th ed.). Wiley.

Couret, J. (2012, May 8). Regents introduce University of North Georgia. *Atlanta Business Chronicle.* https://www.bizjournals.com/atlanta/ news/2012/05/08/regents-introduce-university-of-north.html

DiMaggio, P. J., & Powell, W. W. (1983). The iron cage revisited: Institutional isomorphism and collective rationality in organizational fields. *American Sociological Review, 48*(2), 147–160. https://doi. org/10.2307/2095101

Durant, M. W. (1999). Managing organizational change. Credit Research Foundation. http://citeseerx.ist.psu.edu/viewdoc/download?doi=10.1.1.178.3706&rep=rep1&type=pdf

Harman, K. M. (2002). Merging divergent campus cultures into coherent educational communities: Challenges for higher education leaders. *Higher Education*, *44*(1), 91–114. https://doi.org/10.1023/A:1015565112209

McLeod, S. F. (2017). *Adoption of governance, risk management, and compliance practices in higher education information technology* [Doctoral dissertation, University of Georgia]. https://esploro.libs.uga.edu/esploro/outputs/doctoral/Adoption-of-governance-risk-management-and-compliance-practices-in-higher-education-information-technology/9949333442202959

Morphew, C. C., & Hartley, M. (2006). Mission statements: A thematic analysis of rhetoric across institutional type. *Journal of Higher Education*, *77*(3), 456–471. https://doi.org/10.1353/jhe.2006.0025

Toma, J. D., Dubrow, G., & Hartley, M. (2005). The uses of institutional culture. *Association for the Study of Higher Education (ASHE) Higher Education Report, 31*(2).

Tuckman, B. W. (1965). Developmental sequences in small groups. *Psychological Bulletin*, *63*(6), 384–399. https://doi.org/10.1037/h0022100

University of North Georgia. (2014). *Engaging UNG: Strategic plan 2014–2019*. https://ung.edu/strategic-plan/uploads/files/ung-strategic-plan14-19.pdf?t=1650845185421

University of North Georgia. (n.d.). *30-county UNG service area*. https://ung.edu/government-relations-economic-development/service-area.php

Välimaa, J. (2008). Cultural studies in higher education research. In J. Välimaa & O.-H. Ylijoki (Eds.), *Cultural perspectives on higher education* (pp. 9–25). Springer.

Advancing Transfer Together: How Consolidation Brought Together the University of North Georgia and the National Institute for the Study of Transfer Students

Anna Holcomb, Maggie Segnitz, and Janet L. Marling

At the University of North Georgia (UNG), student transfer is more than an institutional policy; it is woven into the cultural patchwork spanning five campuses located in the state's northern region. The University's approach to transfer, or the movement of students and credits between institutions, is the fortuitous convergence of President Bonita Jacobs's arrival to the North Georgia mountains and the unveiling of consolidation plans by the University System of Georgia (USG). This decision brought together two institutions with a long history of transfer collaboration and set in motion a new relationship that is changing the transfer student experience at UNG and beyond.

Prior to becoming UNG's 17th president, Bonita Jacobs had established herself as a pioneer in transfer advocacy, having founded the National Institute for the Study of Transfer Students (NISTS) in 2002 while serving as Vice President for Student Development at the University of North Texas (UNT), where transfer students comprised 52% of the student body (University of North Texas, 2002). She left UNT in 2011 to become North Georgia College & State University's (NGCSU) first female president with no plans to move the NISTS. However, when it was announced that her institution would be one of four pairs in Georgia to consolidate, Jacobs knew there was an opportunity to advance both NISTS and what would become the University of North Georgia by relocating the organization. Fast forward 10 years, and UNG and NISTS share in milestone anniversaries in 2022—a sesquicentennial for UNG, and NISTS is celebrating 20 years of service to higher education.

A New National Organization for the Forgotten Student

At the turn of the millennium, as global economies grew increasingly interconnected, American students flocked to higher education as a result of the college-for-all movement, eager to join the ranks of knowledge workers (Handel & Williams, 2012; Rizvi & Lingard, 2010). Jacobs found herself in the trenches of this enrollment surge at UNT, a regional public research institution in the Dallas-Fort Worth Metroplex. At the time, there were 22 community college campuses within a 50-mile radius of UNT. Jacobs discussed the dynamic between campuses during this period of influx: "Transfer numbers were going up. Community colleges had grown. They [community colleges] were looking at that transfer mobility, and yet, at the same time there wasn't a lot of hand holding between the two-years [colleges] and four-years [universities]." Recognizing the upward trend in student mobility, Jacobs went in search of literature, best practices, and training to better support the transfer students in her region, only to come up empty-handed—and she was not alone.

Despite the growing regularity of students moving between campuses in their pursuit of a college degree, transfer students were all but forgotten, comprising an invisible presence in the higher education landscape. During the time of NISTS's infancy, Jacobs found very little scholarly work had been written to guide UNT's approach to student transfer. The search for a conference to learn about transfers in a professional community was also unsuccessful. Jacobs recounts, "There really wasn't anything [available]. So I said, 'We're going to do a transfer conference!'"

In February of 2002, Bonita Jacobs, Janet Marling, and their UNT colleagues designed and delivered the inaugural NISTS conference. Over 300 professionals from more than 39 states and Canada convened at UNT. With modest advertising for that first annual gathering, the response was astounding. Jacobs's vision provided a critical space for networking amongst diverse stakeholders with common struggles, answering a call for collaboration between community colleges and four-year institutions in service of transfer and student mobility. Jacobs spent the next nine years shaping NISTS into the singular national organization focused exclusively on transfer education, research, and advocacy.

NISTS's New Home at UNG

During the 2011–2012 academic year, as Jacobs was transitioning to her new institution in North Georgia, NISTS was evolving into a well-respected national organization from its homebase at UNT under the leadership of its second executive director, Janet Marling. As Jacobs and Marling gained footing in their respective leadership endeavors, neither could have predicted the opportunity that was about to knock: USG unveiled consolidation plans for NGCSU and Gainesville State College (GSC).

While Jacobs was not made aware of the consolidation plans on the horizon before taking office, she proved to be just the woman for the job due in no small part to her background as NISTS's founder and first executive director. Recollecting her leadership during the process of consolidation, Jacobs shared, "[A significant] concern with the consolidation was that I would not understand the two-year mission. . . . I did a lot of consulting with two-year schools. I get it. I have great respect for the two-year mission."

Prior to consolidation, GSC offered both associate and bachelor's degrees, with many students completing courses with the goal of transferring to another institution. Frequently, NGCSU was the receiving institution for transferring students. Joining the two institutions expanded educational access to students across the North Georgia region and provided a unique opportunity for students to pursue multiple degree pathways within the same institution.

Recognizing the incredible opportunity consolidation presented for student mobility in the North Georgia region which is further detailed in Chapter 5: *Successful Cultural Outcomes from the UNG Consolidation: Information Technology, Libraries, University Relations* (Crowe et al., 2023). Jacobs helped NISTS relocate its operation to the Dahlonega Campus in August 2012, just as UNG was poised to become a regional powerhouse. As NISTS's host university, UNG had the opportunity to position itself as a trailblazer in educating transfer professionals and advance the university's mission to develop students into leaders for a diverse and global society.

Melding Complementary Transfer Missions

During a consolidation, the administrative process of joining operations, leadership and governance, and resources managed by the separate institutions has visible outcomes. Less tangible, however, is the nurturing of different cultures, weaving the mission and values of each campus into a single unified vision. In the formation of UNG, the developing culture of transfer advocacy is a tapestry constructed from the legacy of GSC's transfer tradition, NISTS's mission to empower transfer champions, and the unique personality of each of the distinct campuses that comprise the institution.

Chaudron Gille, UNG's Provost and Senior Vice President for Academic Affairs, speaks to GSC's commitment to enabling transfer from her perspective as the college's Associate Vice Provost for Academic Affairs at the time of consolidation:

> Gainesville State College had bachelor's degrees, but we were primarily a transfer or two-year school. We were very proud of the foundation that we provided for students in the core curriculum. We were the main supplier [of transfers] to North Georgia College & State University. We also had a lot of students that would go to UGA and Georgia State. We had a steady stream of students that went to Georgia Tech, where there is the Regents' Engineering Transfer Program.

GSC worked diligently to provide students with a solid academic footing before transferring.

While GSC focused on preparing students to transfer out, the culture of transfer at NGCSU centered in its role receiving students completing a bachelor's degree. As UNG would now offer both associate and bachelor's degree programs under one institutional umbrella, consolidation expanded opportunities for students transferring in, out, and between UNG campuses. As Gille explained, "[At an] institution our size, serving a region as large as ours, transfer is a key component." She continued, "That's an important service for us to provide for the region and is an important component of *who we are*." Consolidation expanded pathways for associate-level students in the North Georgia region to transfer in pursuit of a bachelor's degree. UNG's commitment to serving the public good underscores the university's approach to not only create transfer opportunities but also ensure the transfer landscape is navigable for students.

During the process of consolidation, the internal transfer process was established, forming pipelines with transparent requirements for students to transition from associate-level campuses to bachelor's-conferring campuses. Gille explained that this culture of transfer advocacy requires constant calibration to ensure pipelines and programs are maintained and supported in collaboration with partner institutions: "I like to think of us as part of an ecosystem of higher ed[ucation] in this part of the state. Our relationship with our technical college and private sector institutions, as well as other USG institutions, is very important." UNG's holistic view, coupled with the deliberate decision to foster a strong internal transfer culture, demonstrates how student mobility has been a priority for UNG since consolidation.

Tan Tonge, a student from the North Georgia region, exemplifies the success a student can obtain when the student "ecosystem" is nurtured at an institutional level. Tan first attended UNG as a dual enrollment student at the Gainesville Campus before transferring to the Dahlonega Campus for his first year of college with an engineering degree in his sights. Tan remembers this point in his college journey: "I knew I wanted to get into engineering, but I didn't really know the path to get there." Tonge found direction in the Regents' Engineering Pathway, attracted by the myriad transfer opportunities to complete his degree should his top choice of attending Georgia Tech not come to fruition. While Tonge did ultimately graduate from Georgia Tech, he credits both institutions for his success: "I am very proud of the path that I have been on. In fact, in my cubicle [at work] I have a Georgia Tech flag, and then I have a UNG one." UNG's commitment to its multidimensional role in transfer, whether as a student's graduating university or a stop along the journey, provides students like Tan Tonge multiple pathways to achieve their goals.

A New Vision for Transfer Student Support

Consolidation presented an urgent need for UNG to contend with student mobility in the region, and fostering a multidirectional transfer culture was vital to the success of the merger. Jacobs emphasized how UNG's transition support initiatives are centered in the student experience: "We're in the business of graduating students, and that means we need to understand all the different pockets of students; we need to understand that population and what they need to have a successful transition." At UNG, the needs of a growing and diversified transfer student population are met with an innovative approach to support transfer students with targeted outreach and engagement strategies.

Associate Dean of Students and Director of Nighthawk Engagement and Student Transitions (NEST) Darcy Hayes has played an important role in the development and expansion of transfer-related services since consolidation. Jacobs described NEST as a single point of entry for transfer students, one location to access all the transfer-specific resources and information students might need. A successful transfer process is contingent on the student's understanding of how their academic credits will be used toward the degree requirements at their receiving institution. Recognizing the need to build student understanding, NEST collaborated with the Office of Academic Advising to analyze onboarding processes for incoming students on all campuses. Identifying the success of advance scheduling for first-year students, creating a first-semester schedule under the guidance of an academic advisor who is knowledgeable in the student's program of study, the practice was expanded to new incoming transfer students of all majors. Transfer students' academic credits are articulated by the Registrar's Office and reviewed by an academic advisor. As transfer students are often ready for upper-level courses upon entry at their new institution, advance scheduling provides an institutionalized mechanism to meet student needs and streamline academic progress.

NEST also houses transfer experts who are dedicated to advancing transfer student advocacy across all campuses. Hayes shared, "these are professionals who are leading or chairing committees and are looking for student success in their specific populations." UNG's transfer specialists' programmatic portfolio includes transfer student orientations, transfer student success workshops with campus partners, and NEST's flagship offering: the transfer coach program. The transfer coach program offers a differentiated approach that respects the vast educational experiences transfer students may have upon matriculation into UNG. Prospective and incoming transfer students are provided with personal onboarding experiences, and the coaches communicate with transfer students throughout their transition, providing mentorship and a network of peers upon enrollment.

Avalee Vernon Miguel, a current UNG student and transfer coach, exemplifies the success of the program. Reflecting on her experience in the transfer coach program, Miguel shared, "UNG is doing a great job, just taking the time to really appreciate and to welcome their transfer students. This is the first school that I have had this experience with." As an adult learner, Miguel was considering transferring from Chamberlin School of Nursing to UNG to complete her degree. Miguel was uncertain if going back to college to pursue a nursing degree was still the right path for her. In counsel with the Offices of Admission and Academic Advising on the Gainesville Campus, Miguel considered her options beyond the medical field and discussed her transfer credits in the context of a discipline better aligned with her interests. UNG's academic advisors helped Miguel build a plan to complete her bachelor's degree in communications and organizational leadership, igniting her academic momentum, while the transfer coach program helped subdue common transfer student anxieties. Miguel acknowledges that UNG's transfer approach—a combination of peer mentorship, a welcoming culture, and organized academic planning—was vital to her successful transition. Avalee Vernon Miguel now brings her rich personal experiences to her own work as a transfer coach, exemplifying the reflexive nature of UNG's transfer services.

Cultivating Professional Transfer Champions

Not only is UNG responding to student-level needs but also NISTS's presence on campus has elevated UNG's position in the graduate education landscape. Through the Post Master's Certificate in Transfer Leadership and Practice, the only academic program of its kind, UNG is leading the way in preparing higher education professionals to advocate for transfer students at the systemic level. This collaboration between NISTS and UNG's College of Education is building a cadre of individuals well-versed in transfer students, research, policy, and transfer-focused practice so certificate graduates may assume leadership roles within their institutions, communities, and organizations to effect change that levels the educational playing field for a considerable number of students. The program continually strives to ensure that the lack of transfer scholarship and practice, once identified by Jacobs during NISTS's inception, is no longer prohibiting institutions from improving the transfer student experience.

Navigating Emerging Challenges

Maintaining a healthy transfer program requires a nimble approach, facilitating constant recalibration to meet student needs amid shifting regional priorities and national trends, particularly as the effects of the global pandemic continue to ripple throughout higher education. Gille specifically highlighted the loss of institutional knowledge during "The Great Resignation" as a challenge to maintaining transfer pathways that rely on collaboration with partner institutions.

Additionally, increasing mobility in the labor force, coupled with population decline, will result in college-goers tending less and less to be "traditional" college-aged students (Cepeda et al., 2021). Gille explains how emerging trends prominently position transfer advocacy in the future of higher education:

> We know that students are very mobile, and that it is common for them to attend a variety of institutions . . . pressures on the labor force also mean that people are stopping in and out more frequently. The ability to evaluate what someone brings to the institution and give as much credit as possible, and flexibility around that, is going to become increasingly important for all of us.

Furthermore, UNG's 30-county service region mirrors the national picture where many adults have *some* college and no degree, presenting an opportunity for UNG to provide best practices as higher education makes space for nonlinear paths in degree obtainment. From its established position at UNG, NISTS will be there to support these efforts to reengage "stop-out" transfer students to help them achieve their educational goals.

The Future of Transfer at UNG and Beyond

Through consolidation, repositioning the leading change agent in NISTS, and perfectly placed leadership in President Jacobs, UNG has fostered a notable culture of transfer advocacy, yet there is more work to be done. The future is ripe for creating transfer collaborations and alliances between institutions across the North Georgia region, the state, and beyond to develop curricular pathways that allow students to move more seamlessly toward degree completion.

In the 20 years since its first conference, NISTS remains the sole organization exclusively dedicated to empowering practitioners, faculty, and administrators to be transfer champions who challenge the status quo to improve the transfer student experience. Inclusive of two- and four-year institutions and higher education organizations across sectors, NISTS ensures transfer professionals are equipped with the tools and inquiry-based information necessary to serve their transfer student populations. A transdisciplinary approach, robust conference curricula, and practical resources have positioned NISTS as the prominent higher education organization for transfer advocacy.

As student transfer and credit mobility continue to rise across the higher education landscape, the unique partnership of UNG and NISTS will respond. UNG's commitment to transfer will continue to expand across campuses, academic departments, and support services. Similarly, NISTS is broadening its higher education reach while refining its impact. As UNG and NISTS continue to build on the synergy of their relationship and shared commitment to student-centered efforts, the future is bright to advance transfer *together*.

References

Cepeda, R., Buelow, M., Jaggars, S., & Rivera, M. (2021). Like a freshman who didn't get a freshman orientation: How transfer student capital, social support, and self-efficacy intertwine in the transfer student experience. *Frontiers in Psychology*. doi: 10.3389/fpsyg.2021.767395

Handel, S. J., & Williams, R. A. (2012). *The promise of the transfer pathway: Opportunity and challenge for community college students seeking the baccalaureate degree.* New York, NY: College Board Advocacy & Policy Center. Retrieved from http://advocacy.collegeboard.org/sites/default/files/community-college-transferpathway-summary-5938.pdf.

Rizvi, F. & Lingard, B. (2010) *Globalizing education policy.* Routledge, Abingdon, UK.

University of North Texas Office of University Planning. (2002). *Fact Book 2001–2002.* University of North Texas. Retrieved from https://institutionalresearch.unt.edu/sites/default/files/fact_book_2001-2002.pdf

Fulfilling the Potential of Authentic Community Engagement

Andrew J. Pearl

In 2010, North Georgia College & State University (NGCSU) was among the first public institutions in Georgia to receive the Elective Classification for Community Engagement from the Carnegie Foundation. The achievement of classification signaled a commitment to developing mutually-beneficial community/university partnerships and affirmed the institution's public good mission. This dedication was continued after the consolidation of NGCSU and Gainesville State College (GSC) in 2013, and the newly established University of North Georgia (UNG) inherited the elective community engagement classification. To build a shared sense of identity among the recently consolidated institutions across multiple campuses, the 2014–2015 academic year was designated the Year of Engagement at UNG. The Year of Engagement initiative concluded with a series of focus groups that led to a white paper that identified areas for further clarification and growth, including developing a common language and approach and reinforcing the scholarly rigor of community engagement. The commitment to community engagement was also affirmed in UNG's 2014–2019 Strategic Plan, which emphasized community engagement and specifically called for maintaining the Carnegie elective community engagement classification in the 2020 cycle, a goal that was met.

Community engagement is embedded in the culture of UNG, previously and uniquely existing at both NGCSU and GSC prior to consolidation. However, UNG serves a wide variety of diverse communities, and while all five campuses shared an ethos of community engagement, a one-size-fits-all approach would not be effective. A new initiative from Campus Compact, a national coalition of colleges and universities dedicated to the public purposes of higher education, provided UNG with an excellent opportunity to further refine and describe a comprehensive community engagement approach.

In 2015–2016, Campus Compact celebrated its 30th anniversary and invited member presidents and chancellors to sign an action statement that reaffirmed a shared commitment to the public purposes of higher education and a promise to develop a Campus Civic Action Plan to realize those purposes more fully (Campus Compact, 2021). In 2016, President Bonita Jacobs joined as a signatory on the action statement, and soon thereafter, the process of developing UNG's Civic Action Plan began. In 2018, UNG became the first higher education institution in Georgia to complete and submit a Civic Action Plan.

Campus Compact's Civic Action Planning process is centered around five civic commitments toward which member institutions are encouraged to work with "renewed dedication, focus, and vigor":

- We **empower** our students, faculty, staff, and community partners to co-create mutually respectful partnerships in pursuit of a just, equitable, and sustainable future for communities beyond the campus—nearby and around the world.
- We **prepare** our students for lives of engaged citizenship, with the motivation and capacity to deliberate, act, and lead in pursuit of the public good.
- We **embrace** our responsibilities as place-based institutions, contributing to the health and strength of our communities—economically, socially, environmentally, educationally, and politically.
- We **harness** the capacity of our institutions—through research, teaching, partnerships, and institutional practice—to challenge the prevailing social and economic inequalities that threaten our democratic future.

- We **foster** an environment that consistently affirms the centrality of the public purposes of higher education by setting high expectations for members of the campus community to contribute to their achievement. (Campus Compact, 2021)

While these five commitments serve as the guiding framework for the Civic Action Plans, Campus Compact encourages members to "go bold" as they develop their plans and to focus on making the plans meaningful and contextualized to their individualized needs and community partners.

To develop UNG's Civic Action Plan, which would lead directly to preparation for the 2020 cycle of Elective Classification for Community Engagement, UNG's Office of Research and Engagement initiated the formation of a Civic Action Planning Committee with representatives from each of UNG's five campuses (as well as individuals serving university-wide) that included tenure-track and non-tenure-track faculty members from multiple disciplines, and staff members from various administrative units. The committee also purposefully included individuals who had worked at NGCSU and GSC prior to consolidation as well as individuals who had joined UNG post-consolidation.

Contextualizing the Civic Commitments at UNG

The process of creating UNG's Civic Action Plan began with a series of engaging conversations on how UNG embodied and sought to further embed each of the civic commitments. Through connecting to the larger extant literature on community engagement, UNG composed five commitments for UNG and offered contextualized descriptions.

Commitment One: Empower

When the Carnegie Foundation established the elective community engagement classification, they provided a definition that has become a standard-bearer for the field:

Community engagement describes collaboration between institutions of higher education and their larger communities (local, regional/state, national, global) for the mutually beneficial exchange of knowledge and resources in a context of partnership and reciprocity. (Carnegie Elective Classifications, n.d.)

The Carnegie Foundation's definition emphasizes the importance of building community/university partnerships that extend beyond traditional notions of service and outreach. These partnerships value how the knowledge, expertise, and wisdom can be paired with the knowledge and resources of the institution in the spirit of co-creation.

UNG strives to work in partnership with multiple stakeholders and seeks to be a community of students, faculty, staff, alumni, and community partners who are committed to educational excellence, leadership development, and community engagement. This culture is supported regionally through five campus communities, globally through the Institute for Leadership and Strategic Studies and the Center for Global Engagement, and through the Corps of Cadets as a senior military college. Building the necessary institutional infrastructure allows for the facilitation of effective and intentional mutually beneficial, reciprocal, and transformational partnerships that seek to address pressing social, civic, economic, and ethical issues—like access to education and workforce readiness—rising to meet the call outlined in the *Crucible Moment* report for reinvestment in civic learning to produce "informed, engaged, open-minded, and socially responsible people" (National Task Force on Civic Learning and Democratic Engagement, 2012, p. v).

Commitment Two: Prepare

UNG seeks to be an engaged institution that is responsive to the needs of students today and in the future (Kellogg Commission, 1999). As such, the Wingspread Statement of Student Civic Engagement served as inspiration for the second civic commitment (Long et al., 2001). The Wingspread Statement resulted from a gathering of students who were asked to share their civic experiences in higher education, and they affirmed the following points:

- We view democracy as richly participatory rather than procedural; the work of negotiating difference is the work of democracy;
- We recognize and seize opportunities to put our community service activities in context;
- We see ourselves as misunderstood by those who measure student engagement by conventional standards that do not always fit our conceptions of democratic participation; and
- We have a clear sense of how higher education can and should change to provide an environment more conducive to civic education.

As a state-designated leadership institution, UNG takes great responsibility to prepare and motivate students as leaders for a diverse and global society. Examined in Chapter 9 of this book, *The UNG Honors Program: A Commitment to Student Engagement, Service, and Scholarship,* Burger et al. share community engagement projects connecting honors students in experiential learning with their communities. Through a variety of experiences such as service-learning, internships, study abroad, community service, and leadership development opportunities, students gain an understanding of their ability to affect positive change in ways authentic to who they are, build essential skills that propel them into lives of engagement, and become critical thinkers who learn to identify community needs and develop strategies to address critical social issues.

Commitment Three: Embrace

Operating on five campuses and directly serving a 30-county area, UNG has the potential for serving as a true anchor institution in the North Georgia region. According to the Anchor Institution Task Force (AITF) learning community (n.d.), an anchor institution can be thought of as an enduring organization that can provide stability to a locality, particularly with regard to local economies and widening social disparities. Anchor institutions contribute to local community and economic development and are informed by core values like collaboration and partnership, equity and social justice, democracy and democratic practice, and a commitment to place and community. In this spirit, UNG can serve as a truly place-based institution that maximizes and leverages its resources for deep and lasting social change (Yamamura & Koth, 2018).

Each of UNG's campuses embraces the responsibility to fully appreciate and understand the unique economic, social, environmental, educational, and political needs and opportunities within their service area. For example, the community surrounding the residential Dahlonega Campus in the foothills of the Blue Ridge Mountains is a substantively different context that the residential Cumming Campus and its close proximity to Atlanta. This nuanced approach enables UNG to develop a supportive and holistic community/university approach to engagement in order to build and sustain partnerships for a more vibrant community, committed to providing innovative opportunities for scholarship and service.

Commitment Four: Harness

In addition to defining community engagement for the elective classification, the Carnegie Foundation also provides an explanation of the purpose of community engagement, which is:

> to enrich scholarship, research, and creative activity; enhance curriculum, teaching and learning; prepare educated, engaged citizens; strengthen democratic values and civic responsibility; address critical societal issues; and contribute to the public good. (Carnegie Elective Classifications, n.d.)

This definition aligns with Boyer's (1990; 1996) reconsideration of scholarly work, which culminated in his vision for the role of institutions of higher education in society:

> Colleges and universities are one of the greatest hopes for intellectual and civic progress . . . I am convinced that for this hope to be fulfilled, the academy must become a more vigorous partner in the search for answers to our most pressing social, civic, economic, and moral problems, and must reaffirm its historic commitment to what I call the scholarship of engagement. (Boyer, 1996)

As an institution committed to providing a culture of academic excellence, UNG recognizes that engagement is not simply a benevolent act. Engaging with community partners allows for both intellectual and civic progress, as Boyer affirms, and provides a new lens through which to view teaching, research, and service. Infusing a community-engaged approach provides new pathways to discovering and disseminating new knowledge, and UNG works to fully realize, recognize, and reward the strengths of its faculty, staff, students, and community partners. For example, the Office of Academic Engagement offers two annual awards to celebrate the work of engaged faculty and staff members: the Best Practices in Service-Learning Award and the Scholarship of Engagement Award.

Commitment Five: Foster

In 2010, the Executive Committee of the Association of Public and Land-grant Universities' (APLU) Council on Engagement and Outreach commissioned a white paper on the central role that engagement scholarship should have in higher education (Fitzgerald et al., 2012). This white paper included several recommendations, including that higher education must adopt new approaches in order to move engagement from the margin to the mainstream of its research, teaching, and service; and in order for engagement to become fully embedded into the central core of the institution, an ethos of engagement must cut across the missions of teaching, research, and service; be reciprocal and mutually beneficial; and embrace the process and values of civil democracy.

UNG is well-positioned to affirm the centrality of community engagement and to create purposeful alignment of organizational goals that are included in the performance metrics at the unit, college, department, and individual levels. Therefore, the UNG Civic Action Plan was intended to serve as a living document that is regularly accessed, referenced, and updated by students, faculty, staff, and community partners.

Charting a Course for Community Engagement at UNG

UNG's Civic Action Plan concludes with a series of ambitious goals that are purposefully aligned with the institutional values of excellence, student-focus, integrity, engagement, and service. The first stated goal is to increase the profile and celebration of community engagement activities through purposeful opportunities to connect the campuses with their communities. Each of these opportunities would be open to students, faculty, staff, and the community. Next, the Civic Action Plan calls for the formation of a community of practice for faculty and staff members focused on community engagement. A community of practice will be purposefully aligned with the existing Liberal Education and America's Promise (LEAP) initiative at UNG. The third goal is to explore the resources required to expand community engagement efforts at UNG, followed by the fourth goal: to evaluate and identify areas of improvement for the data collection and assessment practices for community engagement. Next, the committee specifically calls for establishing deeper relationships across UNG as a whole to ensure that community engagement plays a central role in the identity of the institution overall. To ensure community engagement truly cuts across the entire institution and speaks to all members of the UNG community, the sixth goal calls for working with deans of students, campus Student Government Associations, and leadership on each campus to determine an appropriate pathway for the civic education and mentoring of students in a way that leverages existing efforts, advocates for incorporating civic learning to appropriate co-curricular activities, and identifies areas of needed programming. The final recommended goal was to determine critical issue areas that help UNG focus its community impact efforts. The Civic Action Plan was written with the acknowledgment that these were ambitious goals that would help to more fully entrench UNG as a truly community-engaged institution.

Conclusion

UNG is an institution with a great deal of potential, both tapped and untapped, for truly engaging with and co-creating a positive impact on a wide range of diverse communities in its service area and beyond. Incredible partnerships exist on each of the five campuses that are positively impacting the lives of community members, students, faculty, and staff. However, this work will only persist to the degree that the institution as a whole prioritizes the importance and centrality of community-engaged work. The

Civic Action Plan is a document that can serve as a roadmap, but unless the goals and recommendations are implemented and assessed for their effectiveness, UNG will not fully realize its engagement potential. Receiving the Elective Classification for Community Engagement in the 2020 cycle is a testament that UNG is well on its way toward demonstrating its excellence in engagement, and joining the prestigious Engagement Scholarship Consortium further solidifies the commitment of leadership to developing future student leaders through authentic engagement in their communities.

References

Anchor Institution Task Force (n.d.). *What is the Anchor Institutions Task Force (AITF)?*. Marga, Inc. https://www.margainc.com/aitf/

Boyer, E. L. (1996). The scholarship of engagement. *Journal of Public Service and Outreach, 1*(1), 11–20.

Boyer, E. L. (1990). *Scholarship reconsidered: Priorities of the professoriate.* Carnegie Foundation for the Advancement of Teaching.

Campus Compact (2021). *Campus Compact Action Statement of Presidents and Chancellors.* https://compact.org/cap/actionstatement/

Carnegie Elective Classifications (n.d.). *The 2024 Elective Classification for Community Engagement.* https://carnegieelectiveclassifications.org/the-2024-elective-classification-for-community-engagement/

Fitzgerald, H. E., Bruns, K., Sonka, S. T., Furco, A., & Swanson, L. (2012). The centrality of engagement in higher education. *Journal of Higher Education Outreach and Engagement, 16*(3), 7–28.

Kellogg Commission on the Future of State and Land Grant Universities (1999). *Returning to our roots: The engaged institution.* NASULGC.

Long, S. E., Saltmarsh, J., & Heffernan, K. (2001). *The new student politics: The Wingspread statement of student civic engagement.* Campus Compact.

National Task Force on Civic Learning and Democratic Engagement. (2012). *A crucible moment: College learning and democracy's future.* Association of American Colleges & Universities.

Yamamura, E. K., & Koth, K. (2018). *Place-based community engagement in higher education: A strategy to transform universities and communities.* Stylus.

UNG's Dual Enrollment Program: Growth Reflecting Institutional Mission of Access

Chaudron Gille, Imani K. Cabell, and Katherine Rose Adams

Dual enrollment provides opportunities for high school students to take postsecondary courses and earn concurrent credit toward both a high school diploma and a college degree. With the expansion and increase in dual enrollment programs nationwide, dual enrollment and access to early college for high school students have gained the attention of state legislatures and educational leaders across the nation. As of 2020, 47 states, including the District of Columbia, have some type of dual enrollment statute or regulation governing one or more common statewide dual enrollment policies (Spencer & Maldonado, 2021).

The University of North Georgia's (UNG) dual enrollment program is the second largest in the University System of Georgia, serving 1,500 students from 140 high schools in about 45 counties. The program engages students on each of the university's campuses, through online coursework and at select off-site locations. The growth of the program in the years since the establishment of a consolidated UNG in 2013 has resulted from the university's reputation for academic excellence, strategic moves by the university, and changes in state policy.

History of Dual Enrollment in Georgia

Dual enrollment has existed in various forms in Georgia since the 1990s. Prior to 2004, dual enrollment was limited to high school juniors and seniors and, more importantly, was supported through the local school district's Quality Basic Education (QBE) funding (Lee, 2019). Under this model, enrollments in the program were low, and dual enrollment was viewed primarily as an opportunity for exceptional students to attend college early. In 2004, the funding model changed. Funds from the Georgia Lottery were used to pay student tuition, and the eligibility criteria were expanded to include ninth and 10th graders, thereby resulting in the benefit of greater student participation as high schools no longer had to bear the full cost.

In 2013, a revised funding model was introduced, administered by the Georgia Student Finance Commission (https://gsfc.georgia.gov/), which ensured that, in addition to paying students' college tuition, the state's QBE funding formula for public high school included dual-enrolled students in their Full Time Equivalent student count (Lee, 2019). Prior to this change, high schools often promoted their Advanced Placement (AP) opportunities to students over dual enrollment so they could receive full state funding for each student. Also, high school teachers were sometimes reluctant to have their strongest students leave their classrooms for dual-enrolled opportunities. In addition, students who took AP classes received a slight benefit in their high school GPAs, a calculation which had implications for class rank and the determination of high school valedictorian. The revised legislation changed the GPA calculation so that AP and dual enrollment courses were on equal footing. While the state law permitted students in ninth, 10th, 11th, and 12th grades to participate in dual enrollment, each postsecondary institution was granted jurisdiction to set their own entrance requirements.

Another government initiative around this time had a major impact on dual enrollment. In August 2011, Governor Nathan Deal announced the launch of Complete College Georgia (CCG) (https://completega.org/) in order to expand the number of Georgians with a postsecondary credential and educate the workforce that Georgia needed for economic development. Widely cited statistics from a 2011 study by Georgetown University predicted that by 2025, 60% of all jobs in Georgia would require some form of postsecondary credential (Carnevale & Rose, 2011). In 2011, only 42% of Georgians had a college degree. The initiative begun by Governor Deal had five areas of focus:

1. College Readiness: mending the P-12 pipeline so that more high
   school students graduated and were ready to begin college
2. Improving Access and Completion for Underserved Students
3. Shortening Time to Degree
4. Restructuring Instructional Delivery
5. Transforming Remediation (CCG, n.d.)

The University System of Georgia, the Technical College System of
Georgia, and private universities and colleges in the state all came together
toward the Complete College Georgia initiative. Governor Deal convened
representatives from all institutions for the launch. Each institution was
charged with developing its own plan to improve access and graduation
addressing the five areas of focus, using data to inform their plans, and
collaborating with community stakeholders.

UNG's Decision to Grow Dual Enrollment

UNG decided to address the P-12 pipeline component of Complete
College Georgia through innovative programming for dual enrollment and
the recruitment of academically strong high school students. Dual enrollment
traditionally consists of top-tier students in Georgia high schools. Hence, it
was perceived as a recruitment opportunity to reach out to accomplished
high school students through the creation of appealing incentives, such as
on-campus college classes. By further growing the program, UNG needed
to establish their brand and decide dual enrollment's purpose and function.

At the time of the 2013 consolidation, North Georgia College & State
University and Gainesville State College each participated in the state's
College Credit Now program, offering Accel and Move on When Ready
(MOWR) (Georgia Department of Education, 2022). Accel's purpose was
to provide a smoother transition from high school to college by offering
meaningful and challenging academic experiences to qualified students,
while MOWR sought to allow an early start to students' college careers.
With Accel, a high school student could receive both high school credit and
college credit for a single course, as well as elect to attend college courses
part time or full time. MOWR was designed for high school juniors and

seniors who took all of their courses at a college and who attended full time. The two programs had different entrance requirements and different funding models. As a result, there were four different enrollment paths for program students with four separate criteria: two different Accel entrance requirements at the associate and baccalaureate levels and two different MOWR entrance requirements at the associate and baccalaureate levels. The application process was cumbersome, and messaging was confusing for students, thus creating barriers in student recruitment and retention.

In 2015, the Georgia Department of Education collapsed the two programs, along with the HOPE Grant, into one program with one funding source (Mealer, 2015). At UNG, this led to a single path to admissions for dual enrollment students at the baccalaureate level. As Gainesville State College and North Georgia College & State University were going through the process of consolidation during this time, the first Complete College Plan for either institution was submitted as a unified UNG plan. The initial team was composed of Maryellen Cosgrove, Chaudron Gille, Bob Michael, Richard Oates, Kris Roney, and Billy Wells. Kris Roney and Chaudron Gille served as the primary authors of the plan. In the initial state-level discussions of "Shortening Time to Degree," the emphasis was on giving credit for prior learning and improving transfer and articulation agreements in order to minimize the loss of credits. However, the emphasis on the P-12 pipeline and the desire to improve access to a college degree for underserved students quickly resulted in the notion of dual enrollment as a means to shorten students' time to degree. UNG's plan consequently included growing its dual enrollment program as one of the institutional strategies to shorten time to degree.

Stages of Program Development

As UNG sought to balance resources with student programming outcomes, as well as work as a newly consolidated institution that previously had disparate programming, multiple models for dual enrollment were constructed. The institution had previously accepted dual-enrolled students to its campuses, but it began receiving requests from area high schools to offer classes on their sites. The initial efforts were with high schools from

East Jackson and Barrow counties. UNG faculty traveled to the high schools, thus initiating UNG's engagement with off-site dual enrollment locations. One goal of the off-site locations was to select locations that would facilitate opportunities to serve multiple high schools under one UNG umbrella. Another goal of the off-site locations was to allow students the opportunity to not only connect on a social level but also enhance their educational opportunities and grow academically with other students. Several different counties were considered for the creation of the off-site partnerships. These partnerships needed to benefit both the university as a pipeline for recruiting students and the school system by providing a connection between the K-12 system and the university system. However, having sufficient enrollment in the classes to support the cost of instruction became an issue, and UNG wanted to distinguish itself as a dual enrollment partner. UNG wanted to provide a richer practice that embodied the college experience by moving students from traditional high school classrooms to college campuses and/ or local college and career academies.

UNG's experience working with Oconee County high schools reinforced the idea that the experience on the college campus was the preferred model. Due to space constraints on the UNG Oconee Campus, an effort was made to place college credit-bearing classes at the high schools with students enrolled from both institutions; however, the high school students did not sign up for those courses; instead, they chose courses on the UNG Oconee Campus. These previous experiences informed UNG's subsequent efforts on the Gainesville and Blue Ridge campuses. Both campuses had strong community support and benefitted from UNG's strong academic reputation as well as its tutoring, testing, and advising resources. Other opportunities, like eCore and online course offerings, provided rural students with greater course selection, opening additional pathways to participation.

The Hall County School System and Jackson County School System partnered with UNG to provide students with off-site opportunities for dual enrollment. The Hall County off-site campus became Ivester Early College, and the Jackson County off-site campus became Empower College and Career Center. Each of these off-site locations provided a unique experience by bridging multiple high schools from their respective counties in one location. UNG faculty members traveled to the site location and held firm to the academic standards set forth by the main university campuses. Each off-site location came with a specific memorandum of understanding, ensuring that policies and procedures of the dual enrollment program would be upheld.

UNG's Academic Advising Model for Dual Enrollment

At UNG, the quality of the program directly relates to the holistic college experience of the student. UNG was determined to provide students with a developmental advising model that centered on student growth and aided in the somewhat cumbersome transition from high school to college. Folsom et al. (2015) defines developmental advising as a style of advising in which the advisor focuses on multiple aspects of a student's skills—such as rationality, behavioral awareness, interpersonal interactions, and problem-solving skills—to help them address challenges. Brenda Perry, UNG's first academic advisor dedicated for dual enrollment, spearheaded the development of UNG's first dual enrollment advising program. At the time of consolidation, Charles Bell became the Dual Enrollment Program Coordinator. UNG's dual enrollment program existed on four campuses with about 253 enrolled students. Under Bell's leadership, dual enrollment saw an increase in enrollment of almost 200 students each year. Further, the program attracted increased interest from additional counties, private schools, and accredited and unaccredited homeschool programs.

During UNG's post-consolidation phase, the demand for additional course offerings became apparent. Pressure to grow the dual enrollment program ignited the need for additional professional staffing roles that focused primarily on dual enrollment. By the fall of 2014, each of UNG's campuses had a designated academic advisor who worked directly with the dual enrollment population. The academic advising department was and is led by the Executive Director of Academic Advising, Terri Carroll. Carroll's role, in part, consists of supporting staff and training dual enrollment advisors to navigate the nuances of working with the dual enrollment population.

Additionally, a new role was designed to manage and advise off-site locations in conjunction with the dual enrollment coordinator. Associate

Vice President and Dean of University College, Carol Adams, took on a new role supervising the dual enrollment off-site locations. Adams was charged with communicating with department heads to acquire faculty for specific course offerings that were being taught at the off-site locations. She also worked with the dual enrollment coordinators to add course offerings to the site locations as needed. Lastly, Adams's role was to be a liaison for faculty and high school partners who had questions, concerns, and/or issues.

The Dual Enrollment Coordinator role continues to evolve with the growth of the program. The coordinator became the program's main face and a pillar of the communities supported by UNG. The role requires going into local high schools, presenting information on dual enrollment, and providing additional support resources for high school counselors and prospective students. Due to the multiple job responsibilities assigned to the dual enrollment coordinator, the role transitioned to an assistant director position in spring of 2019. Imani Cabell became UNG's first Assistant Director for Dual Enrollment. UNG's active advising model centers around providing students with support and direction towards degree attainment. This model helps dual enrollment students to not only take classes for credit but also better understand how these courses can help them acquire a degree.

UNG's Dual Enrollment Program Today

As a result of the growth and success of dual enrollment programs across the state of Georgia, recent legislative changes have curtailed funding for dual-enrolled students. The program allows students to take 15 credit hours per semester, and a maximum of 30 credit hours can be covered by the state. These changes provide students with additional structure and intentionality to their course selections. Along with covering the cost of tuition, the State of Georgia—in partnership with participating universities—also covers the cost of textbooks and university fees for dual enrollment students up to 30 credit hours.

As of fall 2021, UNG's dual enrollment program has seen immense growth in both popularity and student enrollment. The program numbers for the fall 2021 semester consisted of 1,571 students enrolled across five UNG campuses, online, and at two off-site locations. Each student who enters UNG's dual enrollment program meets with their specific dual enrollment advisor for a one-on-one course registration session; prior to the start of the semester, they also meet for a group orientation session. Dual enrollment orientation and advising sessions provide opportunities for new students to gain important information about the college process, support resources, and required courses necessary to meet high school graduation requirements. During that same fall 2021 semester, university officials were impacted by the challenges of the COVID-19 pandemic. Institutions faced challenges in enrollment and student participation. Dual enrollment became a valuable resource for students impacted by COVID-19, as it provided them the option of online college courses as well as face-to-face and hybrid options, while some of their local high schools had to embrace online learning.

Establishing the Reputation of UNG's Dual Enrollment Program

Dual enrollment programs can serve as a guide in navigating the transition from high school to college. If our faculty were only sent into the high schools, students would not gain the experience of navigating a college campus and potentially lose out on adjusting to a more rigorous learning environment. UNG has established unique structures to distinguish its dual enrollment programming by focusing on quality, accessibility, and pipeline recruitment. Even through the growing popularity of dual enrollment, UNG has assuaged concerns about academic rigor by focusing on preparedness, quality, and integrity. It developed policies to accept only high school juniors and seniors, in reflection of student readiness; create program assessments to certify academic success of participation; and establish minimum academic standards. For example, UNG policy states that students must maintain at least a 2.5 college level GPA as well as complete 67% of all their attempted courses to stay eligible for the dual enrollment program. These academic standards are important for not only developing quality students but also maintaining academic rigor within individual programs. UNG's dual enrollment program has met expectations of college-level performance by engaging credentialed faculty and having a rigorous college-level curriculum. Also, UNG developed exceptional academic advising specific to dual-enrolled students and created strong liaisons and relationships between the high schools. Moreover, it added online dual enrollment courses in order to serve more diverse student populations, transportation considerations, and high school partnerships, thereby supporting flexibility and access. Approximately 30% of UNG's dual-enrolled high school seniors matriculate to the university, a percentage higher than the national average. Hence, UNG's dual enrollment program prepares a significant number of students each year, giving them generally a more seamless transition into college life.

Conclusion

UNG's dual enrollment program has gone through different iterations over the years in response to policy changes from the state. The program's popularity has also required the development of new internal processes and guidelines. Changes have come in the way of personnel and funding models; what has lasted over time, though, are the growth of the program and the support for students. The transition from high school to college can be one of the most impactful times of a young student's life, and UNG's dual enrollment program strives to make that challenge less intimidating by providing students with understanding and support for the college transition process.

References

Carnevale, A. P., & Rose, S. J. (2011). *The undereducated American.* Georgetown University Center on Education and the Workforce.

Complete College Georgia. (2022, April). The University System of Georgia. https://completega.org/

Folsom, P., Yoder, F., & Joslin, J. E. (2015). *The new advisor guidebook: Mastering the art of academic advising.* Wiley.

Georgia Department of Education. (2022, April). *Dual Enrollment Program.* https://www.gadoe.org/Curriculum-Instruction-and-Assessment/CTAE/Pages/Transition-Career-Partnerships.aspx

Georgia Student Finance Commission. (2022, March). https://gsfc.georgia.gov/

Lee, J. (2019). Dual enrollment explained. *Georgia Budget & Policy Institute.* https://gbpi.org/dual-enrollment-explained

Mealer, G. (2015, July 14). *The new move on when ready dual enrollment program.* Presentation for the Georgia Association for Career and Technical Education. https://www.gadoe.org/Curriculum-Instruction-and-Assessment/CTAE/Documents/New-MOWR-2015-GACTE.pdf

Spencer, G., & Maldonado, M. (2021). Determinants of dual enrollment access: A national examination of institutional context and state policies. *AERA Open, 7.* https://doi.org/10.1177/23328584211041628

The UNG Honors Program: A Commitment to Student Engagement, Service, and Scholarship

Amy Burger, Royce Dansby-Sparks, Danielle E. Hartsfield, and Stephen Smith

Established on the Dahlonega Campus in 1995, the University of North Georgia's (UNG) Honors Program is committed to developing "a community of academically motivated students who seek opportunities to enhance their learning experience" (UNG Honors Program, 2022). The UNG Honors Program has a special focus on student engagement, defined as involvement in the learning process both in and beyond the classroom (Groccia, 2018). Further, the program encourages active participation in community service as well as scholarship, including involvement in undergraduate research, which aligns with recommendations from the National Collegiate Honors Council (2017). In keeping with this volume's theme, this chapter highlights the ways in which current Honors Program students and recent graduates have excelled in the program's three main facets of student engagement, community service, and scholarship.

Student Engagement

The Honors Program attracts high-achieving students and asks them to maintain academic excellence, promoting engagement throughout their undergraduate experience. Ultimately, this engagement carries over into students' futures. The Dean of Honors, Anastasia Lin, says "the program's most successful students take advantage of every opportunity afforded to them to enhance their trajectory toward their goals." That is, students get out of the Honors Program what they put in, starting with their coursework.

Honors courses facilitate engagement among students by allowing them to take smaller, discussion-based classes that are more rigorous than non-honors sections and encourage the development of critical thinking and independent study skills. Outside the classroom, recent honors graduate Gina Diodati says the Honors Program connects students to "a network of charitable organizations [and] conferences at which they can present their research." Honors students participate in community service and leadership activities both on and off campus and may also engage with a broader scholarly community by attending conferences and sharing their research, which we will address further in subsequent sections of this chapter. Students like Bailey Bullard, a 2022 graduate, value this extracurricular experience: "If it were not for the Honors Program, there are many great academic opportunities such as summer research programs and attending research conferences that would not have been brought to my attention." Honors students also benefit from intellectual collaboration, which Lin characterizes as "a community of scholars similarly dedicated to academic inquiry." Through the program, students make connections with each other and between course materials and their personal interests, increasing their investment in their education. The influence of this commitment to intellectual excellence is evident; on average, honors students have higher GPAs than eligible students who do not participate.

The Honors Program is more than academics to many students. Honors alumna Winolee Furtney says that the program "helped me feel like I was a part of something." Fellow alumna Dena Bosten agrees, saying participating in Honors helped her "be plugged in to something more than academics." The Honors Program cultivates community for students across campuses through monthly meetings and social events. Additionally, in Dahlonega, students who live on campus can choose to live in a dedicated honors hall, and all students have access to an honors library that serves as a lounge and is used by many students as a gathering place. Honors alumnus Sawyer Henderson explains, "the Honors Program forced me to get to know my (now) friends closely in the smaller class sizes and just chatting daily in the honors lab/lounge." As these comments suggest, the Honors Program offers social connectivity as well as opportunities for academic engagement.

Students' commitment to the Honors Program goes beyond their time at UNG. The Honors Advisory Council, a volunteer group of alumni and community members, works to support current students. One of the group's functions is fundraising, which can provide scholarships, fund research, support student attendance at conferences to present their work, and help pay for study abroad. For example, some of the funds raised by the council during the program's 25th anniversary campaign in fall 2020 went toward purchasing supplies and lab equipment needed for students' research projects.

Additionally, Lin notes that "one of the key goals of the Honors Program is supporting students in reaching their academic and professional goals." The Honors Advisory Council contributes to this effort by hosting a career event each spring that connects students to a network of alumni who volunteer to advise students to support their professional development. Many of the professionals who participate are Honors Program alumni themselves. Many alumni think fondly of their time in the program, too. Honors Advisory Council member Heather Deweese says joining the Honors Program "might have been the best decision I made as a student."

Service

Participation in community service is another key facet of the Honors Program. For example, new students in the first-year honors seminar course participate in a variety of volunteer opportunities around campus and the city of Dahlonega, which we describe next. We follow with profiles of several current students and recent alumni who have exemplified a commitment to service.

HNRS 1000 First-Year Seminar

Volunteerism has recently been embedded in HNRS 1000: *Introduction to Honors Academic Inquiry*, a seminar course for first-year Honors Program students. Since fall 2021, each student in HNRS 1000 has completed 10 hours of service to UNG or the Dahlonega community. This service component is the result of a new partnership between the Honors Program and UNG's Appalachian Studies Center. Students in the fall 2021 semester had several service opportunities from which they could choose, including volunteering at Mount Hope Cemetery, Hometown Harvest food pantry and community garden, and Lumpkin County Schools.

The HNRS 1000 students who volunteered at Dahlonega's historic Mount Hope Cemetery in the fall 2021 semester were involved in several projects. Under the guidance of a leader from the Dahlonega Cemetery Committee, they learned new skills, such as how to safely clean grave sites and make headstone rubbings to preserve text and artwork faded by time. Autumn Sniffen, a student in the course and a member of the Class of 2025, recognizes the value of this work, noting, "Usually we think of preserving history in a figurative sense, as in just not forgetting it, but in reality, if you don't clean a tombstone, you eventually won't be able to read it, and its story will be lost forever."

Some Mount Hope volunteers were involved in a fall clean-up day, while others participated in the work of marking the unmarked grave sites of Lumpkin County's African American citizens, including graves of individuals who were once enslaved. Jesse Kronen, who volunteered at Mount Hope throughout the fall 2021 semester, was thankful and reflective of his experience and noted the duality of "learning about the history and community of the wonderful town I now study and live in, but I feel I was able to become a small part of that history through the restoration work I did there." Classmate Kathleen Daly concurred on the impact of gaining skills while giving back, noting, "There is a peace in Mount Hope, the site plays a huge part in Dahlonega's history, and it was such an honor to do my part in preservation!"

Other students opted to volunteer at UNG's Hometown Harvest food pantry; these students stocked donations and helped visitors find needed items. Saara Anam, a first-year Honors student in the fall 2021 semester, explains what the experience meant:

> After volunteering at the food pantry, my sense of community was greatly impacted and strengthened as I felt a part of something bigger than me. The Hometown Harvest food pantry truly cares for the well-being of Dahlonega residents and UNG students by providing a safe

space for people who are less fortunate than others, and I am grateful to have positively contributed to that.

Saara's classmate and fellow food pantry volunteer, Scott Fitz Gerald, agreed, "The food pantry helps students get basic supplies so that they can focus on other aspects of life. I love volunteering at a place that provides for the community's needs."

Some students served at the Hometown Harvest community garden located at the historic Vickery House. The garden not only supplies the food pantry but also provides fresh produce to children attending Lumpkin County Schools and offers educational programs for students from kindergarten through 12th grade, essentially serving as an outdoor classroom. In addition, some first-year honors students worked with the school nutrition director at Lumpkin County Schools to plan educational field trips for elementary children.

Notably, the HNRS 1000 students connected their community service work to their semester-long research projects. For example, students who volunteered at Mount Hope engaged in research about funerary art or notable Lumpkin County citizens buried at the cemetery. In this way, students could appreciate how community service could inform their scholarship and vice versa. The students' research projects culminated in an academic poster session attended by fellow students and faculty, and their posters were on display at Dahlonega City Hall for several months in 2022, allowing them to share their research findings with a broader audience. The service component of the HNRS 1000 course not only empowered first-year students to become involved in their community but also represented the Honors Program's commitment to service and the development of civic-mindedness among its students.

Student Profiles

While community service is embedded in the Honors Program through the HNRS 1000 course, students are encouraged to maintain their involvement in service as they continue in the program. Several current students and recent alumni have made long-term community connections through their service work. We share some of their stories to illustrate how honors students exemplify a dedication to serving the community.

Abigael Bell is a current honors student majoring in kinesiology and minoring in Spanish. Bell started community service in high school, leading a community-wide effort to sponsor a Peruvian child and raising enough money to pay for the child's food, school, and health care for nine years. She also became heavily involved in teaching children on Sundays for her hometown church, an activity she has continued as a college student through a Dahlonega church. As a high school senior, she volunteered at a paralysis recovery center, where she found her calling for occupational therapy (OT); Bell says working with people who have been disabled and seeing them recover function "is so rewarding . . . I love it." In pursuit of more experience to prepare for that career, Bell has volunteered weekly at Benchmark Physical Therapy, where she assists Jen Hoyt, the staff OT, with a wide range of patients. "Being part of this . . . is so amazing," remarks Bell.

Natalie Macy, a 2021 biology graduate, was heavily involved in community service, acting as a Habitat for Humanity officer from her sophomore year until her senior year (and as president for the last two) and working with the Jeremiah's Place free clinic. She led by example, helping with build sites, assisting with Habitat's store, and manning the clinic's front desk (run by Community Helping Place). The latter experience directly connected to her career plan, which is to finish medical school and practice neurology. She did several fundraisers, but she gained most from her direct involvement in the local community working alongside volunteers from the local affiliate as well as the people receiving Habitat homes. "Learning a lot, meeting new people, and seeing students get engaged" in the community were a few of the ways Macy feels she benefited from her service experiences. She has always loved Habitat's mission and feels good about being able to contribute to their success in Lumpkin County.

During her time at UNG, Dana Robison, a 2020 psychology graduate, was involved in many student organizations, but the one thread that ran through not just her undergraduate years but the two years since graduation has been the Family Connections program. She responded to an appeal for volunteers during her first month at UNG and immediately took a liking to helping a young student cope with difficulties (both emotional and academic). Robison recalls "feeling like I really belonged" in the community shortly after beginning her service as a mentor in the middle school. She has mentored two students during her time with the program, visiting with them weekly throughout the school year to help them with school or visit and do artwork. She delights in their successes and helps them cope with their setbacks, even if it means "doing an embarrassing dance for a TikTok video." She says that mentoring has been fulfilling for her in part because she was jealous of kids who had such mentoring opportunities when she was younger: "I can almost heal in a way" by going back into the schools and "being that person for someone else."

Scholarship

Honors Program students are encouraged to seek real world application of their learning and out-of-the-classroom experiences. The high impact practices of scholarship and undergraduate research have been a hallmark of the honors experience. While representing less than 1% of the general student population, honors students were involved in over 25% of the student research presentations and posters at the UNG Annual Research Conference in 2021. For the last 10 years, all Honors Program students have been required to participate in an honors thesis or capstone experience as a graduation requirement. Honors students are also overrepresented in nominations and awards for nationally competitive scholarships and external summer research experiences for undergraduates.

One such alumna, Jasmine Williamson, had a stellar research progression as an honors student and McNair Scholar before earning her degree in biology in 2018. When she arrived on campus, Williamson missed her friends at the University of Georgia and had thoughts of transferring. With some encouragement, she persisted in the Honors Program at UNG, eventually finding her stride and landing in the ecology research lab of Jessy Patterson and David Patterson. "They worked with me tirelessly for years," remembers Williamson. Her thesis work involved the study of the effects of abiotic factors on salamander diversity and ecology at UNG's Hurricane Creek research site. On the day of her thesis defense, the room was packed with supportive faculty who had watched her develop at UNG. Williamson's honors thesis research work was eventually published with her as primary author in the *Georgia Journal of Science* (Williamson et al., 2020).

In fall 2020, Williamson presented a talk on her undergraduate research experience in the Honors Program with the next generation of honors students just starting their own research journey in HNRS 3000: *Honors Research Methods*. She later applied for the highly competitive National Science Foundation Graduate Research Fellowship Program and in spring of 2021, on the third attempt, became UNG's fourth student and third honors student to obtain the coveted fellowship worth $138,000 in funding for graduate research. "Once I was awarded the fellowship, I had opportunities to do really impactful graduate research all over the country," says Williamson. "Of course, as an amphibian nerd, I chose a program where I could continue studying salamanders" Williamson is now pursuing her Master of Science degree in wildlife science in the Department of Fish, Wildlife, and Conservation Sciences at Oregon State University, studying how local habitat changes due to wildfire and timber harvest effect plethodontid salamander occupancy and abundance.

Hailey Rueden, a 2022 psychology graduate, has also thrived in undergraduate research during her time in the program. Rueden joined the Honors Program at the end of her first year at UNG. As such, she missed many of the opportunities to earn honors credits for core curriculum courses. However, that did not deter this highly self-motivated student. She jumped right in, seeking honors credit in two psychology courses, one a contract course that she had to develop individually with guidance from a faculty member to earn honors credit in a non-honors course. It was in this semester that she also met her instructor, Amanda Halliburton, who would eventually become her honors thesis chair and research advisor. The next spring semester, as part of HNRS 3000, Halliburton worked with Rueden to develop a proposed research plan to study factors that influence the unequal diagnosis rates for attention deficit hyperactivity disorder between males and females. They tackled the arduous task of seeking approval from local school systems to administer an institutional review board (IRB) approved survey on a sensitive topic to local schoolteachers. Rueden was able to endure the challenges that are inherent to the complexities of this type of research. This high level of planning and engagement in undergraduate research—developing, executing, and defending a complex study—is commendable and a hallmark of what it means to be a distinguished Honors Program graduate from UNG.

In addition to the honors thesis experience, Rueden has completed several honors contracts to earn individualized honors credit in several courses by incorporating separate undergraduate research projects. In the spring 2022 semester alone, she proposed two separate contracts that involved creating surveys requiring IRB approval, implementation, data analysis, and final written research reports. As a testament to her amazing work ethic, she was able to complete this additional work during a single semester and during a time she was finishing work on her honors thesis. After Rueden demonstrated her aptitude for undergraduate research, she was invited to participate with several faculty researchers in another timely research project investigating the impact of COVID-19 on stress and mental health of college-aged students. The study (Halliburton et al., 2021) was published with Rueden as a student co-author before she graduated. It should come as no surprise that Rueden has been accepted into at least one clinical PhD program in psychology and has interviews at several others. While Rueden and Williamson represent two highly successful students who had access to superior undergraduate research mentoring, all honors graduates are exposed to the high impact practice of undergraduate research during their time in the program, and many gain acceptances to graduate programs, job placements, and publications partly because of their experiences in the program. Honors students and their research mentors have the option to publish their honors thesis work on the UNG Libraries database (https://digitalcommons.northgeorgia.edu/honors_theses/).

Conclusion

As these profiles of current students and recent graduates indicate, the Honors Program offers numerous opportunities that empower students to excel. Honors students engage with their peers at UNG and within their professional and academic disciplines through specialized coursework and networking opportunities, participate in various service endeavors to support the local community, and immerse themselves in scholarship both in and out of the classroom, often presenting and publishing their work to audiences beyond UNG. We are incredibly proud of the accomplishments of the hundreds of honors students who have graduated since the program was first established more than 25 years ago. And while we celebrate the achievements of honors students today, we also keep an eye toward the future as new generations of students enter the program and make their mark at UNG, the community, and the world beyond.

References

Groccia, J. E. (2018). What is student engagement?. *New Directions for Teaching and Learning, 2018*(154), 11–20. https://doi.org/10.1002/tl.20287

Halliburton, A. E., Hill, M. B., Dawson, B. L., Hightower, J. M., & Rueden, H. (2021). Increased stress, declining mental health: Emerging adults' experiences in college during COVID-19. *Emerging Adulthood, 9*(5), 433–448. https://doi.org/10.1177/21676968211025348

National Collegiate Honors Council. (2017). *Basic characteristics of a fully developed honors program.* https://www.nchchonors.org/uploaded/NCHC_FILES/PDFs/NCHC_Basic_Characteristics-Program_2017.pdf

UNG Honors Program. (2022). *Honors Program.* University of North Georgia. https://ung.edu/honors-program/

Williamson, J., Bailey, A., Lougee, J., Patterson, D., & Patterson, J. (2020). A preliminary investigation of the impact of forest management practices on microhabitat abiotic variables in the southern Appalachian Mountains. *Georgia Journal of Science, 78*(2). https://digitalcommons.gaacademy.org/gjs/vol78/iss2/13

Serving Students by Serving Faculty: The Beginnings and Futures of UNG's Center for Teaching, Learning, and Leadership

J. Michael Rifenburg and Roger Runquist

In this chapter, we survey the past, present, and imagined futures of the Center for Teaching, Learning, and Leadership (CTLL). CTLL is a faculty-facing center that supports the mission, vision, and values of the University of North Georgia (UNG) through strengthening the service, research, and teaching of UNG's over 2,000 faculty. While the 20,000 UNG students may never know CTLL exists or may never enter its virtual or physical office spaces, the CTLL staff, CTLL faculty fellows, and all faculty who connect with CTLL do so out of a deep commitment to strengthening education for all students. We begin with CTLL's past and give a special thanks to Chaudron Gille, Irene Kokkala, and Mary Carney, who all served as past directors and played instrumental roles in shaping CTLL and who contributed their written remembrances of CTLL.

CTLL Past

Prior to consolidation in 2013, both the North Georgia College & State University (NGCSU) and Gainesville State College (GSC) institutions had developed teaching and learning centers. At GSC, Gille directed CTLL from 2004 to 2010. When Gille assumed leadership of GSC's CTLL in 2004, the center's existing programming provided new faculty and staff orientations as well as mentoring on the tenure and promotion processes. The center also provided pedagogical training to help new faculty hires hone the teaching skills necessary to transition successfully to the classroom. Gille led the redesign and expansion of these programs into a New Faculty Academy that included a common book, monthly topics, and online modules; faculty who completed the program would receive certificates and permanent increases to their base salaries. CTLL also offered a Staff Excellence Program: staff members who completed 10 professional development activities could, like faculty, earn certificates and small bumps in annual salary. The 2008 economic recession presented Gille with budgetary challenges. Gille designed a Professional Development Day as a counter to limited travel funding. This one-day conference featured concurrent sessions for faculty and staff, lunch, and a joint meeting between the college's faculty and the staff council.

North of Gainesville, at NGCSU in Dahlonega, Irene Kokkala founded the Center of Teaching and Learning Excellence (CTLE) in 2005. Kokkala directed CTLE until 2013—the year of consolidation. Kokkala's leadership helped grow CTLE's staff to include an instructional technology and multimedia developer, instructional designer, a part-time administrative assistant and graphic designer, and student workers. Kokkala also had a variety of faculty fellows in areas such as pedagogy, innovative instructional technology, and service-learning.

With this robust staff and faculty fellows in place, CTLE implemented multiple faculty-focused initiatives. CTLE hosted New Faculty Orientation activities, coordinated the Teaching and Learning Excellence Awards, helped develop fully online and hybrid courses, started a Service-Learning Task Force, and supported faculty interested in adopting instructional technologies. CTLE also published *The Teacher*, a quarterly publication that featured faculty's pedagogical and scholarly essays as well as critical and creative writing.

CTLE specifically focused on establishing and supporting best practices in online teaching. For example, CTLE helped faculty become familiar with using the college's learning management system and education technologies like podcasting, video solutions, tablets, and the pedagogical use of virtual worlds.

Under Kokkala's leadership, the Faculty Development Advisory Council (FDAC) and Online Learning Advisory Council (OLAC) supported

CTLE. The FDAC helped organize, coordinate, and sponsor teaching and learning activities for NGCSU's faculty, with the overall focus of creating opportunities for quality innovations in curriculum and instruction. Similarly, the OLAC helped develop and implement online course policies, online course review processes, and incentive programs to support faculty who designed online coursework.

Back at GSC, Mary Carney took over as CTLL director in 2010. Carney oversaw the center through consolidation in 2013. Following consolidation, Kokkala was named director of Distance Education & Technology Integration (DETI). During Carney's tenure, and with the help of Kokkala as head of the Southern Regional Faculty and Instructional Development Consortium (SRFIDC), UNG's CTLL became a leader among centers for teaching and learning within USG. Carney became Advisory Chair and then Chair of USG's Consortium for Teaching and Learning from 2014 to 2016. After consolidation, UNG updated its onboarding process for faculty, and CTLL played a critical role in re-envisioning how faculty were welcomed into the university's culture. Carney developed a multi-campus, multi-day orientation for new faculty.

Carney and her CTLL team established several reading and writing groups that offered space for faculty to gather and to build and share knowledge. For example, what started as a book group soon turned into a cohort of department heads working together monthly to strategize best practices. During summers, CTLL held writing workshops that eventually led to the formation of the Write@UNG initiative led by J. Michael Rifenburg. While leading CTLL, Carney partnered with UNG faculty members to co-author multiple scholarly articles and book chapters related to the Scholarship of Teaching and Learning (SoTL). Carney also founded and served as Editor-in-Chief of *Teaching Academic: A CTLL Blog*. To help UNG faculty advance their scholarship and pursue publication, CTLL partnered with the Human Subjects Research Office to offer a diverse selection of research workshops.

During her time leading CTLL, Carney also spearheaded the Liberal Education and America's Promise (LEAP) initiative in Georgia. This initiative is a part of the American Association of Colleges and Universities (AAC&U), an organization based in Washington, DC, focused on strengthening undergraduate education. In her role as chair of the USG Consortium for Teaching and Learning, Carney fostered the awareness and expansion of LEAP programs by co-leading the opening and concluding workshops of the USG faculty learning community on LEAP. Carney and CTLL's work on LEAP illustrates UNG's and USG's robust commitment to envisioning and coordinating major initiatives focused on supporting student learning. In 2020, following the departure of Carney, Roger Runquist took over as CTLL Director. He has directed the center during the COVID-19 pandemic and the challenges the pandemic is creating across higher education—which is where we find CTLL today.

CTLL Present

CTLL is focused on four primary areas designed to support faculty: teaching and learning; scholarly writing; career milestones; and academic leadership. The first area, teaching and learning, might be the one most familiar to readers who are familiar with centers for teaching and learning across U.S. higher education. This area advances UNG's focus on excellence in teaching and learning. Most faculty at UNG teach what is called a 4/4 load, teaching four courses in the fall and four courses in the spring. UNG is, therefore, a teaching-intensive university where the bulk of a faculty member's time is dedicated to teaching. Indeed, most faculty are more heavily evaluated on teaching than on any other aspect of their work at UNG (such as research and service). CTLL, then, focuses the bulk of its resources toward supporting faculty instruction by bringing innovative workshops, cohorts, and learning communities to faculty that help them refine their teaching practices and introduce them to innovation in teaching that is backed by research.

CTLL offers a Research-Based Teaching Series (RBTS), which is a regularly scheduled one-hour workshop on teaching methods. During the 2020 fall semester, RBTS facilitators led sessions on how to include service-learning in online courses and how to encourage and teach students to write stronger online discussion posts.

Additionally, CTLL financially supports Teaching Circles. Based on the concept of Teaching Circle as first implemented by Appalachian State

University, Teaching Circles at UNG provide an opportunity for informal and productive conversations among faculty and teaching staff interested in exploring topics related to academic excellence. CTLL provides mini grants to faculty and teaching staff who want to form a Teaching Circle on a particular topic of their choosing. The members of the Teaching Circle organize the logistics of their meetings and provide an end-of-semester report to CTLL summarizing the Teaching Circle's work and how that work supported UNG's focus on academic excellence. Through these teaching and learning programs in CTLL, the emphasis remains on bringing together faculty from across rank, from across disciplines, and from across various campuses. Through community-building and research-based teaching practices, CTLL strives to support UNG's mission of "academic excellence in a student-focused environment" (UNG, n.d.).

Not only does it support faculty in the classroom but CTLL also offers programming to support faculty writing and scholarship. CTLL designed the Write@UNG initiative, under which it offers the Write Now Academy. This application-based one-semester cohort is led by different faculty facilitators. These facilitators help participants through Wendy Belcher's *Writing Your Journal Article in 12 Weeks*, which provides constructive step-by-step guidance on writing an academic journal article. CTLL also provides Friday Writing Sessions, which are one-hour virtual meetings about select topics related to writing, and Shut Up & Write, which as the name suggests, invites faculty to gather, greet each other, and then shut up and write. As with its focus on teaching and learning so also is CTLL committed to creating community through which faculty grow as scholars.

The two additional areas of focus for CTLL are on career milestones. Career milestones look at the overall career of a faculty member and focuses efforts on these various stages. Stages would include retention, tenure, promotion, and post-tenure. CTLL also looks to assist faculty in learning the skills necessary to move into leadership positions as part of their career trajectory.

The professional life of a college professor involves teaching, researching, and serving. CTLL provides wrap-around services to support new incoming faculty—through New Faculty Orientation—and offers services for established faculty who, through career advancement, find themselves shifting to new administrator roles. From the beginning of an academic career to the close of an academic career, CTLL, as a faculty-facing center, intentionally designs and implements programming to build community and support UNG's vision, mission, and values.

CTLL Future

The future initiatives offered by CTLL will be shaped by a variety of influences, such as USG initiatives and priorities as well as the needs of UNG's faculty and students. Funding provided by the state of Georgia as well as university revenue drives the budget of centers such as CTLL which, in turn, has a direct impact on initiatives that can be undertaken.

Each spring starting in 2022, faculty will have the opportunity to participate in a faculty needs assessment survey. Responses on those surveys will help CTLL determine priorities in a variety of areas, including pedagogy, research, and leadership. The survey will also help CTLL assess the preferred workshop modalities as well as meeting times of faculty. As an annual event, the needs assessment should provide an opportunity for faculty to voice what they believe are upcoming needs relating to CTLL programming in a meaningful way.

At the time of this writing (spring 2022), CTLL began piloting a Certified Peer Observation (CPO) program to help improve teaching and to provide another datapoint in the evaluation of teaching. While there are several issues inherent to student evaluations of teaching, the CPO program attempts to provide a non-punitive way of bettering the classroom experience. The peer observers are trained to use a consistent vocabulary and methods during the observation process. The process of evaluation consists of multiple meetings between the faculty member and the observer. These meetings involve a pre-meeting held before the observation, the observation, and a post-observation meeting. The program benefits most from the observation and post-observation meeting's being repeated, which allows for documentation of improved performance. Participants have complete transparency in the process and are provided with evaluation instruments that will be used throughout the process. The final report is presented to the faculty member, who can select to include the document in their promotion and tenure paperwork at their own choosing.

Another new program began in the summer of 2021 when CTLL offered its first Summer Academy. The academy is designed to provide faculty with a time to focus on a specific topic area in the teaching profession. The summer of 2021 focused on student engagement while the 2022 summer academy focused on enhancing faculty writing skills.

Several programs offered at CTLL will continue as well. For example, CTLL will continue to celebrate the achievements of faculty, departments, and programs through their annual awards programs in such areas as leadership, research and creative activities, and teaching. By partnering with entities such as DETI, the Center for Undergraduate Research and Creative Activities, and the Office of Academic Engagement, faculty award offerings are expanded to include areas like engagement and technology. During the last few years, UNG has been well-represented at the state level with the result being top honors from several award divisions. CTLL will continue to recognize the talent of UNG's faculty and the excellent work they are doing.

CTLL will remain involved in helping faculty reach their career milestones, recognizing the importance of promoting and retaining talented faculty. Coordinating and promoting workshops with DETI on the retention and promotion process will continue to play an important part in the CTLL mission. Likewise, CTLL will continue to host New Faculty Orientation to acclimate and welcome new faculty to the UNG community. Beginning in the fall of 2022, new faculty will also have new opportunities to work with a faculty mentor from outside of their home department when they elect to participate in the CTLL mentoring program. Incoming faculty can also continue to learn about a variety of topics and build a community as the New Faculty Institute (NFI) continues to acclimate our new colleagues.

The Faculty Fellows program has transitioned since it was originally conceived by Kokkala and now serves as an important method for outreach at all UNG campuses. These fellows now represent each UNG campus and continually provide great perspectives on what is going on in their classrooms and some creative ways of addressing certain issues, but they also help faculty navigate campus-specific resources and opportunities. Further, faculty can realize support for their research and creative activities through writing programs, such as Shut Up & Write, Writing Academy, Write Now, and participation in a variety of academies, including the High Impact Practices (HIP) Academy and the Scholarship on Teaching and Learning (SoTL) Academy.

Teaching and learning centers like CTLL support and champion faculty throughout their careers and are an important piece to enhancing students' instructional experience. UNG's CTLL will continue to provide an evolving set of programs and enhance its selection of resources to benefit the faculty. The continued success of the faculty and students of UNG will continue to be a driving factor for CTLL.

At the Close

The C at the beginning of CTLL stands for *center*. This well-chosen word fits nicely into the mission and focus of CTLL—an intellectual hub, a center, for faculty to connect and grow in their teaching, their service, and their scholarship. The noun *center* also works because it captures how CTLL is positioned in the internal UNG structures. We are proud to have CTLL described as a *center* and the institutional support and stability that comes from such a designation. As we embrace the center-ness of CTLL, we also encourage faculty and staff and readers of this collection to see the C in CTLL as standing for *community*. When we describe the work of CTLL to people, we find that again and again, we come back to the idea of community. As we reflect on the past, present, and imagined future of CTLL, we see the word community pulsing throughout our programming. Through the coming together of faculty, across rank, campus, and discipline, we strengthen our service, teaching, and research for the students and community members with whom we work.

References

University of North Georgia. (n.d.). *Vision, mission & values*. https://ung. edu/about/mission-vision-values.php

Preparing Cadets for Effective Global Engagement as Army Officers: Global Military Programs at the University of North Georgia

Keith P. Antonia, Anthony D. Fritchle, and Billy E. Wells Jr.

The University of North Georgia (UNG) prizes its federally designated role as one of the United States' six senior military colleges in developing today's cadets for leadership in tomorrow's global security environment. The Corps of Cadets—the Boar's Head Brigade—is a superior leader development program that has been transforming students into highly effective junior leaders for the military and for other public and private enterprises since 1873. The foundation of leadership acquired in the Corps of Cadets has propelled countless graduates to executive leadership in a broad array of professions positively impacting the North Georgia region, the state of Georgia, the United States, and the world.

While the other senior military colleges produce officers for all U.S. military services, this university is unique in that UNG commissions cadets only to serve as U.S. Army officers; therefore, this paper is written from an Army perspective regarding the preparation of cadets for effective global engagement as future officers. According to U.S. Army learning doctrine, "cultural understanding, regional expertise, and language proficiency (CREL) are key enablers that allow the Army to respond globally and engage regionally to conduct joint combined arms operations" (U.S. Department of the Army, 2017, p. 20).

The first section of this chapter briefly provides context to the momentum that CREL gained in Army pre-commissioning education over the last 20 years. The second section describes the effort and resources that UNG committed toward creating opportunities for cadets to develop

CREL. The final section contains conclusions drawn from UNG's global awareness curriculum and co-curricular programing for cadets.

Overview of Army Pre-commissioning in U.S. Higher Education Institutions

There are four sources from which Army officers are commissioned: (1) The U.S. Military Academy (USMA) at West Point; (2) Army Reserve Officer Training Corps (ROTC); (3) Officer Candidate School; and (4) direct commission. Of these, Army ROTC and the USMA are the only commissioning sources within higher education institutions and where Army pre-commissioning education occurs. The focus of this chapter is on the largest commissioning source: Army ROTC. Under the U.S. Army's Cadet Command (USACC), Army ROTC programs are embedded in 274 host universities, many of which have cross-enrollment agreements with other higher education institutions in their geographic areas (South, 2019). Together, these programs were to commission 6,000 Army officers in federal fiscal year 2020 (J. Evans, personal communication, October 3, 2018). These numbers are impactful when one considers that 1,107 cadets were commissioned from the USMA in 2020 (O'Connor, 2020, para. 1). Furthermore, Army ROTC generally produces about 80% of second lieutenants commissioning from U.S. higher education institutions.[1]

Cultural Understanding in Army Leaders

In 2001, the Army Chief of Staff directed the U.S. Army War College to "identify the strategic leader skill sets for officers" (Wong et al., 2003, p. iii) in the post-9/11 environment. Subsequently, the War College's Strategic Studies Institute scholars produced a report in which six "metacompetencies" were identified, one of which was cross-cultural savvy (Wong et al., 2003, p. v). In their report, the authors proposed that education in cross-cultural skills is crucial to the development of strategic-level leaders, and they advocated that such education should begin at the undergraduate level for cadets seeking military commissions. They suggested that subjects and experiences

---

1   These numbers vary each year based on Army requirements.

such as foreign languages, international affairs, regional studies, and study abroad would provide the foundation necessary for strategic leadership.

Years after the Strategic Studies Institute noted the value of officer pre-commissioning education, the Army's Training and Doctrine Command (TRADOC) also emphasized the importance of cultural understanding in Army operations. Fourteen years of war proved "the need for its forces to be culturally aware, culturally empathetic, regionally informed, and to use the appropriate language to facilitate communication and improve understanding with the nation's joint, interorganizational, and multinational partners, and local populations" (U.S. Department of the Army, 2017, p. 22). In addition to Army War College analysis and TRADOC guidance, many other documents and writings emphasize the criticality of developing cultural awareness. For example, Lexie Kadlec (2018) blogged for the National Association of Colleges and Employers about the employability of young people who gained experience abroad. Kadlec noted that employers want to hire future leaders who are adaptive and critical thinkers comfortable connecting with people from other cultures. Kadlec also observed that experiences abroad have become increasingly important in an increasingly globalized world.

Through its cadet programs at the USMA and Army ROTC, the Army responded to the call for pre-commissioning education that provides robust opportunities for cadets to begin developing cultural understanding. For example, the USMA has been expanding their cadet semester abroad program since the early 2000s, so between 2010 and 2017, over 900 cadets studied abroad (Johnson, 2017). In addition, each year the USMA enrolls up to 60 international cadets from eligible countries selected by the U.S. Departments of State and Defense (United States Military Academy, 2021). The West Point Association of Graduates observed that,

> as Army officers . . . cadets will need to be able to adapt to diverse cultures and environments, to live, work, and communicate with different populations, and to understand and consider new and different perspectives. Travel abroad . . . increases cadets' foreign language proficiency, regional expertise, and cross-cultural competence. (Johnson, 2017)

The Army ROTC also acknowledged the importance of developing cultural understanding in Army ROTC cadets. A 2018 U.S. Army Cadet Command pamphlet stated the following:

> Future Army leaders must be capable of operating in complex operational environments throughout the world. To succeed, they must interact with the populace, security forces, governing officials, and others with influence. Leaders must understand how the local culture affects the environment and take this into account when executing military operations. *Cultural awareness training begins during pre-commissioning training* [emphasis added]. (U.S. Department of the Army, 2018, p. 1)

USACC regulations also provide incentives for ROTC cadets to develop cultural competence, including ROTC foreign language scholarships and incentive pay for studying languages that are "of importance to the Army" (U.S. Department of the Army, 2018, p. 22).

Recognizing the educational value of pre-commissioning international education, UNG began to develop and expand opportunities for its cadets to acquire the cultural understanding needed to operate in tomorrow's international security environment. The following section describes UNG's academic and co-curricular programs that contribute to cadet cultural understanding and development. Note that although the Corps of Cadets comprises only 6.44% of the UNG student population, the opportunities that were developed to enhance cadet education were made available to other students at the university.

International Education Programs for UNG Cadets

In 2014, UNG's strategic plan included the following goal from the mission statement: "to develop students into leaders for a diverse and global society" (UNG Strategic Plan, 2014–2019, n.d.). Additionally, an institutional objective stated that "UNG will become a leader in internationalized learning with an emphasis on globalization and the needs of an emerging civilian and military workforce." A strategy to accomplish that objective was to "ensure the military education academic program meets the needs of the next generation of military officers and supports foundational competencies for effective leadership in complex and uncertain environments" (UNG, Strategic Plan, 2014–2019, p. 6). At present, the university's general education (core) curriculum includes coursework that requires all students (including cadets) to "analyze political, cultural, or socioeconomic interactions among people or organizations of the world" (UNG, 2021, 2020–2021 UNG Academic Catalog, General Education section). The strategic plan nested nicely with the aforementioned Army War College Strategic Studies Institute, TRADOC, and USACC ideas of developing leaders prepared to operate in an uncertain future international security environment.

Recognizing the importance of cultural understanding for the Army's future leaders, UNG has been developing organizational structures to support and grow a variety of new programs since the early 2000s. The programs include foreign language offerings and becoming a Mandarin Chinese Language Flagship university; degree programs in international affairs and strategic and security studies; collaborating with the International Military Academic Forum to develop partnerships with European military academies; developing cadet semester exchange programs with foreign military academies; developing faculty exchange opportunities with partner foreign military academies; developing international military internships; encouraging cadet participation in international conferences; and partnering with the George and Carol Olmsted Foundation for grant funding under their Undergraduate Program for Overseas Travel and Cultural Immersion opportunities for cadets. An Institute for Leadership and Strategic Studies was formed in 2015 to identify gaps in cadet education requirements and offerings, and to incubate programs to fill those gaps.

Institute for Leadership and Strategic Studies

To prepare cadets for future leadership challenges, the university created an Institute for Leadership and Strategic Studies (ILSS), led by the university's senior vice president for leadership and global engagement (a former UNG professor of military science) and served by an advisory board consisting of leaders who have an interest in the Cadet Military

Leadership Program and who have senior executive experience in various parts of the world. The ILSS identifies gaps between current academic and co-curricular offerings, as well as organizational structures. The ILSS also works across university divisions to incubate programs that can fill those gaps and enhance cadet military education. One example of a gap was the absence of an organizational structure to create and manage opportunities with international military partners and the U.S. Department of Defense for cadet cultural understanding. The gap was addressed through the establishment of a Global Military Programs Directorate.

Global Military Programs Directorate

The university created a Global Military Programs (GMP) Directorate with a director and an assistant director to maintain and develop partnerships with international military academies, as well as to promote cultural understanding development opportunities—*and their value*—to cadets. The directorate provides services for cadets from foreign military academies visiting or enrolling in UNG's Corps of Cadets, foreign military scholars, and UNG faculty and staff traveling abroad to enhance military education programs and opportunities for cadets. The directorate also provides services for UNG cadets to study, intern, and train with U.S. military entities and foreign military academies and militaries abroad. These programs are described in greater detail in the following sections. However, before delving into more detail on the array of GMP's activities, an example of the directorate's work with the Republic of China Military Academy (ROCMA) in Taiwan is illustrative.

The UNG-ROCMA partnership was formalized with the signing of a Cooperation and Exchange Agreement in 2012 by the president of then North Georgia College & State University (now UNG) and the superintendent of ROCMA. Since then, the agreement was updated in 2018 with an expiration year of 2023 (Memorandum, 2018). An abridged list of activities to which each party agreed illuminates the nature of the partnership:

- Explore opportunities for collaboration in student, faculty, and staff exchange; sharing joint scholarly research for publication; exchange for professional development opportunities; and military training for cadets.

- Enter into written agreements for each of the above activities, which will include identifying academic units and people involved, duration of the activity, and funding.
- Conduct planning and evaluation meetings to review progress.
- Resolve disputes in a friendly manner via consultation and negotiation.
- For cadet semester exchange, each party will [among other stipulations]:
  o Provide course registration assistance.
  o Allow cadets to attend orientation and specified cadet training events.
  o Agree to apply credits earned at the host institution toward the home degree.
  o Generate official transcripts at the end of each semester for outgoing cadets.
  o Provide transportation to and from airports and a room with required cadet furnishings.

The UNG president's and the ROCMA superintendent's personal involvement reinforced the value of this partnership, and the international staffs in both institutions sustain a strong relationship, which ultimately benefits cadets in both countries. This partnership was assessed in 2021 as exceptionally strong, and it has remained a priority since its inception.

Collaboration with the International Military Academy Consortia

To expand its cooperation and outreach in professional military education and training opportunities, the GMP maintains membership in international military academy consortia, including the International Symposium of Military Academies (ISOMA) and the International Military Academic Forum (iMAF). The iMAF is a "European initiative for the exchange of young officers inspired by Erasmus" and is a key ally and partner in cadet and faculty academic mobility, hosted by the military academies in

Poland, Hungary, Romania, Austria, and the Czech Republic (Gell, 2017). Collaboration with these organizations supports UNG's cadet cross-cultural development. The iMAF meets annually in Europe to expand and reinforce the existing cooperation in officer education among its member nations. A program under the iMAF is the Exchange of Military Young Officers (EMILYO), the primary objective of which is to "promote a European Security and Defense Culture":

> In terms of spreading the idea among the Officer Cadets and Students participating in the Basic Officer Education, that current and future challenges can be better managed together. This goes hand in hand with an education for the Union's Common Security and Defense Policy (CSDP). (Gell, 2017)

Several of UNG's partnerships with foreign military academies were formed due to its association with iMAF, as well as several other pathways for collaboration in nearly every category of international military cadet education.

Cadet Semester Exchange with Foreign Military Academies

The GMP directorate established semester exchange programs with several foreign military academies. Through memorandums of agreement, UNG cadets attend foreign military academies for a semester, and those military academies reciprocate by enrolling their cadets in UNG's Corps of Cadets for a semester. The benefits of the military exchange program are obvious. By studying at foreign military academies, our cadets are immersed in the culture and language of those academies. While foreign cadets fully participate in the Corps of Cadets, UNG cadets are introduced to future officers from foreign countries and are, at the very least, familiarized with their cultures and languages. This experience brings reality to the notion of the value of cultural understanding development and internationalization for the U.S. Army's future officers. As of 2021, the GMP directorate has developed formal exchange agreements with service academies in Poland, Taiwan, Hungary, Argentina, Romania, Latvia, Germany, Republic of Georgia, and Korea.

Faculty Exchange with Foreign Military Academies

Another function of the GMP directorate is to collaborate with foreign military academies and ministries of defense to invite military officers and faculty to instruct, guest lecture, conduct research, and/or consult in disciplines such as cybersecurity, strategic and security studies, military science, and foreign language. In the area of research, the GMP coordinates with UNG faculty to support projects that align with foreign government initiatives, and provides liaison with U.S. federal, state, and local agencies. Alternatively, the GMP seeks opportunities for UNG faculty and/or staff to conduct similar activities with foreign service academies.

International Military Internships

Another function of the GMP directorate is to develop and manage cadet internship opportunities with U.S. and foreign military and security organizations.

Examples include internships with the School of the Western Hemisphere at Fort Benning, Georgia; North Atlantic Treaty Organization's (NATO) Defense College in Rome, Italy; and Asia Pacific Center for Security Studies in Waikiki, Hawaii. These internships include activities that achieve specific learning outcomes. For example, the internship learning outcomes expected from the NATO's school in Oberammergau, Germany are the following:

- Understand the NATO administrative, operational, and organizational structure.
- Understand how NATO works jointly to manage operations within the European theatre.
- Work in a multi-national environment and alongside instructors and other foreign military personnel to broaden military cultural awareness and understanding.
- Live and work in Germany; immerse in the German culture.

Internship programs help cadets further develop work-related skills, confidence in working in foreign military environments, and foreign language skills, as well as acquire additional cross-cultural competencies.

Cadet Participation in International Conferences

Many foreign service academies host week-long international cadet conferences on their campuses, and the GMP directorate coordinates to send UNG cadets to these high-impact educational events (see Figure 11.1). One of many examples was the 2018 International Cadet Conference hosted by the National Defense Academy of Japan. Cadets from approximately 25 military academies from all over the world participate in this annual conference, giving our cadets a diverse international experience. Cadets spend a week in the academy's barracks; are escorted by Japanese cadets; and are encouraged to experience Japanese culture, including visits to national heritage sites. During the conference, cadets discuss topics such as United Nations peacekeeping and mission command. One UNG cadet wrote that,

> being surrounded by so many people from different countries was eye-opening...
>
> I learned so much just from talking to these people one on one [sic.]... These conferences are an extremely great learning experience regarding educational exposure as well as increasing global awareness. (B. Wells, personal communication, September 14, 2018)

UNG cadets have participated in similar conferences in the Republic of Georgia, Latvia, Romania, and Poland.

Figure 11.1: UNG Cadets Pictured at the May 2019 International Cadet Conference in Turin, Italy

Note. Photo from Leonard, C. (2020, January 17). Olmsted foundation increases grant to UNG, HBCUs for overseas immersion. *UNG News*. Retrieved November 23, 2021, from https://ung.edu/news/articles/2020/01/olmsted-foundation-increases-grant-to-ung,-hbcus-for-overseas-immersion.php

The GMP directorate provides additional opportunities to attend conferences that are not associated with military academies. One such event was the 2019 Model United Nations (UN) for college students in Menton, France, hosted by the Sciences Po Undergraduate College. World-class speakers address issues in the Middle East and Mediterranean areas. Undergraduate students "hone skills in diplomacy, negotiation, critical thinking, compromise, public speaking, writing, and research" (Model United Nations, n.d.). Another example is in cyber technology (see Figure 11.2). A UNG cadet, a cadet from Spelman College in Atlanta (who was sponsored by UNG), and a UNG computer science faculty member attended the 2019 North Atlantic Treaty Organization's Annual International Conference on Cyber Conflict in Tallinn, Estonia. Professionals from many different countries shared their perspectives on international cybersecurity challenges. The UNG cadet wrote the following:

> This conference is probably the best broadening experience any cadet or aspiring information security specialist can [have] to really be exposed to the realm of cybersecurity and see the perspectives of our NATO allies. Another benefit... is simply meeting the other attendants of the conference [and] networking with U.S. personnel and NATO personnel. There are members from nearly every NATO member country and quite a few U.S. Military personnel, ranging from Officers from Cyber Command to West Point and Naval academy cadets. (B. Wells, personal communication, September 17, 2019)

Figure 11.2: UNG Faculty member, Cadets and Spellman College cadet pictured at the May 2019 NATO Cyber Conference in Tallinn, Estonia

Note. Photo from Leonard, C. (2020, January 17). Olmsted foundation increases grant to UNG, HBCUs for overseas immersion. UNG News. Retrieved November 23, 2021, from https://ung.edu/news/articles/2020/01/olmsted-foundation-increases-grant-to-ung,-hbcus-for-overseas-immersion.php

Foreign Military Training

The Global Military Programs directorate seeks opportunities for cadets to train with foreign countries' military academies or militaries. For example, UNG cadets undertook an 11-day trip to Poland in 2019 to participate in the Annual Military Ski Patrol Competition in Szklarska (see Figure 11.3), which was hosted by the Mountaineering Training Section of the General Kościuszko Military Academy of Land Forces (MULF) in cooperation with the Jednostka Wojskowa Komandosow Military Unit (a Polish military special operations unit). Upon arriving in Poland, UNG cadets were transported to the MULF, given a tour of the academy, and stayed the night. The next day, they traveled to Szklarska, checked into a hotel, and began training on tasks they would accomplish during the competition. The three-day competition took place in snow-covered mountainous terrain and involved cross-country skiing and mountain rescue tasks over a distance of 40 kilometers. Military teams came from Italy, the Czech Republic, and Poland. After the competition, the cadets returned to the military academy and were escorted by Polish cadets to tour historical sites in Wroclaw.

Figure 11.3: UNG Cadets Participate in a Military Ski Patrol Competition in Poland
Note. Photo from Rogers, E. (2018, March 8). Cadets represent U.S. in military ski competition, UNG News. Retrieved November 23, 2021, from https://ung.edu/news/articles/2018/03/cadets-represent-u.s.-in-military-ski-competition.php

International Cadet Week

The Global Military Programs directorate hosts the International Cadet Week (ICW) each November in conjunction with the U.S. International Education Week promoted by the U.S. Departments of Education and State (U.S. Department of Education, n.d.). The UNG ICW provides cadets from foreign military academies with immersive experiences in regional U.S. cultures as well as U.S. military and senior military college cultures. An incidental benefit of the experience is that it fosters personal relationships between UNG and foreign military academy cadets that may prove beneficial in the future if they reconnect later in their military careers. Although the primary benefit of ICW is to strengthen relationships with UNG's foreign military academy partners, inviting cadets from non-partner military academies creates an opportunity to explore the feasibility of expanding partnerships with other nations' service academies. Past ICWs included cadets from Italy, Latvia, Poland, the Republic of Georgia, Japan, Brazil, Korea, and several other countries.

UNG ICW activities include cultural activities both on and off campus. International cadets live with UNG's cadets in cadet residence halls and participate in activities such as attending classes; visiting the U.S. Army Maneuver Center of Excellence at Fort Benning, Georgia; visiting Atlanta, Georgia cultural sites; and participating in a military staff ride, which is a culminating event that focuses on the military leadership and tactical decision-making during the U.S. Civil War Atlanta Campaign and the Chickamauga Battle in Chattanooga, Tennessee.

International Academic Programs

Modern and Classical Language Programs

In the early 2000s, UNG offered bachelor's degrees in Spanish and French and minors in those languages plus German. UNG now offers bachelor's degrees in Arabic, Chinese, French, Spanish, and Russian, and minors are offered in Arabic, Chinese, French, German, Italian, Japanese, Korean, and Russian. Other languages taught are Farsi, Portuguese, and Latin (Languages at UNG, 2021).

UNG's efforts to expand language opportunities for cadets began in 2003 with an initiative to secure academic credit for cadets who were also National Guard soldiers and had completed language training at the Defense Language Institute Foreign Language Center (DLIFLC). Following a UNG faculty visit to DLIFLC in Monterey, California, the university developed an articulation agreement for academic credit. With roughly one third of the Corps of Cadets in the Guard, including those in occupational specialties requiring critical language skills, this articulation agreement was an important first step.

Subsequently, discussions began on how to best move forward with expanding language offerings most pertinent to a military career. Chinese Mandarin was selected as the best choice due to its wide usefulness beyond the military. Then, in 2007, the National Security Education Program (NSEP) fielded Project Global Officer (Project GO) that funded ROTC language programs. UNG was accepted into Project GO in 2008. Three years later, with a strong Mandarin program, UNG was selected by the Department of Defense (DoD) to become an ROTC Chinese Flagship, the only one in the nation. In 2018, the Mandarin program was further expanded to include all students, and the institution became a regular NSEP Chinese Language Flagship. All these programs offered scholarships, in addition to funding for faculty. Most recently, the DoD-funded Cyber Institute includes language scholarships for 20 students enrolled in cyber education programs.

Throughout this effort, the emphasis has been on providing opportunities in languages deemed critical to the DoD, especially Chinese, Russian, Korean, and Arabic. Each of these languages are deemed to be progressively growing critical languages and were offered in stages: from initial offerings, to minors, then to majors. UNG's efforts to expand capability have been exceptionally innovative, including intensive Summer Language Institutes targeted at freshmen, required language immersion abroad for majors, and partnerships with other language instruction entities, such as the Goethe Institute. Additional opportunities continue to increase UNG's capacity and boost the university's internationalization efforts more generally.

Degree Programs in International Affairs and Strategic and Security Studies

Two bachelor's degree programs are popular with cadets at UNG: International Affairs and Strategic and Security Studies programs. The International Affairs degree establishes "a strong theoretical and analytical foundation in international relations" (UNG International Affairs, 2021), and students experience both a study abroad experience and an internship as part of the program. Cadets in the major select a concentration in either North Africa and the Middle East, East Asia, Latin America, or Europe. The Strategic and Security Studies degree program "focuses on the theory and application of intelligence and military power to the construction of national defense policy" in which cadets are "introduced to various aspects of security and . . . have the opportunity to specialize in one of . . . five areas of concentration, including cybersecurity, intelligence, history, international affairs, language, or military science" (UNG Strategic and Security Studies, 2021). A study abroad or international internship is required to complete the degree. Cadets may also major in other fields of study while minoring in International Affairs or Strategic and Security Studies.

Olmsted Foundation Funding

The Cadet Military Leadership Program seeks funding to pay for cadet travel to international military program opportunities, thus providing an additional incentive for cadets to take advantage of these high impact educational activities. An important source of funding comes from the generosity of the George and Carol Olmsted Foundation (Olmsted Foundation, n.d.), which offers an Overseas Travel and Cultural Immersion grant program for cadets at U.S. service academies and senior military colleges. Army cadets who desire to commission into the regular Army into branches that involve combat—or those that support combat—and who exhibit superior leadership ability are eligible. Olmsted Foundation grant funding is managed by the UNG's Global Military Programs directorate and funds cadet travel and expenses to participate in short-duration trips to non-English-speaking countries to attend conferences or military training. Funds may also be used for overseas internships embedded in non-U.S. installations in non-English-speaking countries. In 2018, the Olmsted Foundation encouraged UNG to partner with Georgia State University's Army ROTC program to fund cross-enrolled cadets from three Historically Black Colleges and Universities in Atlanta. These cadets travel with UNG cadets, and they participate together in international experiences (see Figure 11.2).

Conclusion

Graduates are the Corps of Cadets' best credentials. There are abundant examples of cadets who took advantage of the cultural understanding developmental coursework and co-curricular activities, such as those spotlighted in Chapter 12, *The Future of International Education at the University of North Georgia: Creating a Global Learning Environment for all Students* (Schulte & Singh, 2023). A former male cadet who commissioned as an infantry lieutenant hailed from the state of Virginia. The cadet earned bachelor's degrees in International Affairs with a Middle East Concentration, Arabic, and History. The cadet studied abroad in the countries of Oman and Jordan; interned with the North Atlantic Treaty Organization's defense college in Rome, Italy; attended international conferences in Romania and Poland; and was a recipient of the Project Global Officer Scholarship. This cadet was an example of a junior Army officer whose mission was to lead a platoon to close with the enemy by means of fire and maneuver to defeat or capture him, or to repel his assault by fire, close combat, and counterattack. But this lieutenant's application of force was tempered with an understanding of the strategic and cultural environment in which the platoon was operating: a competency of great value to his unit, our allies, and the United States.

Another notable example is a former female cadet from the state of Georgia who earned a bachelor's degree in Chinese with minors in military leadership and global leadership. The cadet participated in the Chinese Language Flagship program and became proficient in the Chinese language, studied abroad at National Taiwan University and Beijing Union University, and interned at a children's museum in Beijing. Upon graduating, the cadet commissioned into the Army National Guard in the cyber branch. Hence, here was a lieutenant who was proficient in Chinese and whose mission was to conduct offensive and defensive cyber operations: a combination of unspeakable value to the U.S. national security effort.

One additional example was a Black male cadet, also from the state of Georgia, who majored in Arabic with a minor in military leadership. He attended the Summer Language Institute for Arabic his freshman year. Later, he studied abroad in Morocco and attended an international conference in Latvia. He commissioned as a regular Army officer in the quartermaster corps and will bring value to Army logistics operations if his unit is deployed to an Arabic-speaking country or when working with the military staffs of Arabic nations.

In all, the statistics demonstrate the emphasis the UNG Cadet Military Leadership Program places on cadet cultural understanding. At the beginning of the fall 2020 semester, there were 738 Army ROTC cadets in the Corps of Cadets. Of those:

- 90 were Strategic and Security Studies majors with concentrations in cyber, intelligence, history, international affairs, language, and military science
- 38 were International Affairs majors with concentrations in Middle East, Europe, Asia, and Latin America
- One was an East Asian Studies major
- 25 were Arabic, Chinese, and Russian language majors
- 27 were minoring or concentrating in Arabic, Chinese, Russian, German, Japanese, Spanish, French, and Korean
- 12 were enrolled in the intelligence minor
- 13 were enrolled in international affairs minors

Seventeen percent of the Corps of Cadets were majoring in a cultural understanding developmental field of study, and many others were enrolled in related minors and concentrations. During the academic year 2018–2019, 77 cadets traveled to 23 different countries for cadet exchange, military-related internships, conferences, military training, and study abroad programs (this number was far less in 2019–2020 due to COVID-19 pandemic travel restrictions). Cultural understanding is also built into the military science curriculum, as well as UNG's general educational curriculum, and is absorbed by cadets interacting with foreign military academy exchange cadets. Since the Corps of Cadets is embedded in UNG's civilian student population, cadets are exposed to the various diverse cultures that comprise the student body, including UNG's undergraduate international student population.

The University of North Georgia recognizes its role as a partner in Army pre-commissioning education to prepare cadets for effective global engagement as commissioned officers. Developing and managing the programs to support the Cadet Military Leadership Program's cultural understanding developmental objective described herein requires a considerable amount of collaboration, coordination for incoming and outgoing cadet exchanges, and personal involvement in receiving and integrating international cadets into the Corps of Cadets each fall and spring semester. The creation of an organizational structure staffed with former U.S. Army leaders who understand military culture has been of tremendous value in growing programs to develop cadets' cultural competencies.

References

Gell, H. (2017). *Implementation group for the European Initiative for the Exchange of Young Officers inspired by Erasmus: Purpose, objectives, achievements & future at a glance.* Theresan Military Academy. http://www.emilyo.eu/sites/default/files/Gell%20History/2017%2012%20 28%20Implementation%20Group%20Objectives.pdf

Johnson, C. (2017). *West Point semester abroad program.* West Point Association of Graduates. https://www.westpointaog.org/file/ development/SuptNEW-Semester-Abroad-single-pages.pdf

Kadlec, L. (2018). How do international experiences make millennials and generation z more employable? *National Association of Colleges and Employers.* https://community.naceweb.org/blogs/lexie- kadlec/2018/03/20/how-do-international-experiences-make-millennials.

Memorandum of Understanding for Academic Cooperation Between the Board of Regents of the University System of Georgia and on Behalf of the University of North Georgia and the Republic of China

Military Academy. (2018, August 27).

Model United Nations. (n.d.). *Welcome to NMUN*. https://www.nmun.org/

O'Connor, B. (2020, June 13). *West Point class of 2020 graduates in historic ceremony*. U.S. Army. https://www.army.mil/article/236475/west_point_class_of_2020_graduates_in_historic_ceremony

Olmsted Foundation. (n.d.) *Overseas travel and cultural immersion*. http://www.olmstedfoundation.org/

South, T. (2019, October 15). *Army ROTC must find more officers than it has in years, and here's how it's happening*. The Army Times. https://www.armytimes.com/news/your-army/2019/10/16/army-rotc-must-find-more-officers-than-it-has-in-years-and-heres-how-its-happening/

University of North Georgia. (2021). About UNG. In *2020–2021 UNG academic catalog*. https://catalog.ung.edu/content.php?catoid=28&navoid=917

University of North Georgia. (n.d.). *International affairs (B.A.)*. https://ung.edu/degrees/bachelors/ba-in-international-affairs.php

University of North Georgia. (n.d.). *Languages at UNG*. https://ung.edu/college-of-arts-and-letters/languages/index.php

University of North Georgia. (n.d.). *Strategic plan, 2014–2019*. https://ung.edu/strategic-plan/strategic-plan-2014-2019.php

University of North Georgia. (n.d.). *Strategic and security studies (B.A.)*. https://ung.edu/degrees/bachelors/ba-in-strategic-and-security-studies.php

United States Military Academy. (n.d.). *How to apply*. https://www.westpoint.edu/admissions/prospective-cadets/international-cadets

U.S. Department of Education. (n.d.). *International education week*. https://sites.ed.gov/international/international-education-week-2020/

U.S. Department of the Army. (2017). *The U.S. Army learning concept for training and education 2020–2040* (TRADOC Pamphlet 525-8-2). Training and Doctrine Command.

U.S. Department of the Army (2018). *Cultural awareness training program* [USACC Pamphlet 145-9-1]. U.S. Army Cadet Command.

Wong, L., Gerras, S., Kidd, W., & Pricone, R. (2003). *Strategic leadership competencies*. Army War College Press.

The Future of International Education at the University of North Georgia: Creating a Global Learning Environment for all Students

Sheila Schulte and Raghvendra Singh

Reimagining Internationalization at UNG through the Center for Global Engagement

The culture of the University of North Georgia (UNG) has embraced and supported internationalization efforts, and these efforts will surely continue into its future. But how will these efforts develop over the coming decades? Can UNG continue to increase student mobility while creating a global learning environment for all students through curricular and co-curricular activities? This chapter reflects on these questions by examining the major themes of education abroad activities, international student recruitment activities, faculty and staff development, and the creation of sustainable partnerships both locally and globally.

The UNG Center for Global Engagement (CGE) was established in 2008. According to the American Council on Education's (ACE's) Internationalization Lab Report (2021), "leveraging the university's military mission and standing as a senior military college enabled UNG to expand its academic programs, international focus, and funding sources for all students at UNG by building upon the foundations established through military programs" (p. 6). Over the years, CGE has developed into a centralized hub for all students on all five campuses that includes the following internationalization activities: education abroad opportunities, international student and scholar services that assist all F and J visa holders with compliance, campus integration and community engagement, and co-curricular programming through partnerships with student clubs and campus units to provide global learning opportunities. UNG participated in the American Council on Education's 17th Internationalization Laboratory cohort. The overall experience spanned over 18 months and finished in January 2021, with a final report outlining the strategies for campus internationalization with the goal of long-lasting institutional change (CGE, 2021).

One of the starting points for reimagining internationalization was to create an institutional definition for global learning, which is a "critical analysis of and an engagement with complex, interdependent global systems, and their implications for people's lives. Through curricular and co-curricular experiences, global learning creates intentional intercultural connections that develop leaders for a diverse, sustainable, and global society" (Office of Academic Affairs, n.d.). At the core of our work is the impact global learning will have on UNG students. Thousands of students have benefitted from CGE's programs since its inception. Several recent examples could be cited. A communications major who moved to North Georgia from El Salvador acquired English skills while in middle and high school and decided to immerse himself in a completely new language (Chinese) for a study abroad experience. An international student from Denmark who cared deeply about climate change decided to step into a leadership role with the Sustainability Club; that role gave her the confidence to run for Student Government Association president. A Human Services Delivery Administration student who, undaunted by the pandemic, took advantage of a new virtual internship abroad opportunity with an Australian company ultimately ended up with a job offer.

These are just a few anecdotes that highlight the opportunities for global learning at UNG. This chapter will synthesize several different emerging themes that result from the ACE Laboratory process and will be essential in creating a greater global learning environment moving forward. These themes include increasing curricular and co-curricular opportunities for global learning, increasing international student enrollment, and creating sustainable relationships with transnational organizations.

Education Abroad at UNG

UNG, like most higher education institutions, strives to provide a broad portfolio of education abroad programs that meet the needs of its student population. These programs are varied in duration, location, and specific learning opportunities (e.g., study, research, internship, or service-learning). While having many available offerings in order to attract broad student interest is ideal, CGE has found that the key to facilitating UNG student opportunities abroad is through academic integration of the education abroad experience into the individual student's plan of study.

Since 2011, the University System of Georgia has been engaged in a statewide initiative between institutions of higher education called Complete College Georgia to improve access and graduation of students in the state of Georgia. While one of the goals of the project was to shorten the period of graduation, one of the outcomes of the project for UNG has been to create plans of study for each major with purposeful academic advising (UNG QEP, n.d.). Another important factor affecting academic planning is that students who are eligible for federal financial aid can only use that aid toward courses within their plans of study (Federal Student Aid, 2021). These are two important reasons for UNG students to plan early and intentionally for their education abroad opportunity.

The term *academic integration* indicates that the university must create education abroad opportunities that fit directly into UNG's academic majors. This may seem elementary, but academic integration involves an intentional approach to education abroad advising, student planning, and, most importantly, cooperation with academic departments. Instead of asking "Where do you want to go?," the first question is "What's your major?" Advising is based on the student's academic plan and their current academic standing. Academic integration can only be accomplished through close collaboration between the academic departments and the CGE to determine which programs meet the course equivalents for the UNG major. This detailed work is reviewed on a regular basis, and, when done well, can greatly assist students in feeling confident that their overseas experience will fit into their plan of study. Overall, this type of intentional academic integration guarantees that the student can continue making progress toward graduation and receive their federal financial aid, all while learning new skills abroad. In the end, this endeavor also places the emphasis on the academics of the activity rather than on the allure of a particular location, putting the "education" back into "education abroad."

Despite these best efforts, only 1.5% of UNG students engage in an education abroad opportunity (CGE, 2021). How can UNG increase global learning opportunities for all students? The answer lies in curricular and co-curricular integration of global learning within our campus settings.

Study Away: Experiential Learning at UNG

One recent addition to the list of high-impact practices at UNG is the opportunity for Study Away at UNG. Study Away provides a short-term domestic study option outside of North Georgia led by a faculty member (UNG's Study Away Program, n.d.). These programs encourage UNG students to take a deeper dive into an academic discipline by using a specific environment or community as the classroom. Study Away allows students to learn by doing, build relationships with faculty, and gain confidence to participate in other types of high-impact practices during their UNG careers. This programming augments the institution's education abroad activities and provides students a way to understand diverse communities and environments within the United States. Program topics include Spanish and Hispanic heritage in St. Augustine, Florida; community development among the North Arapahoe Tribe in Wyoming; and Geosciences with the U.S. National Park Services.

Virtual Engagement through Cooperative International Online Learning (COIL)

Another way to enhance the global learning environment at UNG is to increase the use of virtual learning opportunities with entities outside of the United States. These activities, labeled Cooperative International Online Learning (COIL), create meaningful connections between UNG students and faculty and our international partners. Virtual exchanges were especially useful during the COVID pandemic when travel was not possible, and they remain a key initiative for all students to access international opportunities

(SUNY COIL Center, n.d.). UNG has utilized a broad range of virtual choices: complete courses, course projects, case studies, and language learning. The use of COIL in Chinese language classrooms has also been the subject of a recent doctoral dissertation in the UNG Higher Education and Leadership program (Huang, 2022).

Global Learning Practices at the Local Level

After reviewing existing institutional data as well as collecting new data, the ACE Internationalization Lab's Curricular and Co-curricular Working Group recommended a more institutional approach to global learning at UNG (CGE, 2021). As a result, UNG needs to examine the core curriculum to ensure that global learning outcomes are a part of all courses, not just those designated as fulfilling a "global course" requirement. A core curriculum revision will be forthcoming from the University System of Georgia, and this revision will be an excellent opportunity for UNG to revisit how to embed and expand global learning. It seems prudent to include enhanced faculty training to think about how all courses, despite the discipline, can incorporate a global learning lens. These reflective activities already happen in pockets across UNG campuses, but they would profit from a systemized training approach to global learning. In order to be successful, staff will be included in efforts to ensure that co-curricular activities at UNG align with the mission of promoting global learning. The creation of faculty and staff training to facilitate a global learning environment will mean an investment of financial and intellectual resources, but this investment will pay dividends when UNG students are prepared to work in a complex and interdependent world.

The Future of International Student Recruitment at UNG

According to UNESCO Institute for Statistics (2018), the total number of students who crossed international borders to pursue their education doubled from 2.2 million in 1998 to 5.6 million in 2018. Several push and pull factors have influenced international students to consider the international educational experience. During the past two decades, while there has been fluctuation in international student mobility among the various countries of origin, the United States has remained a leading country of destination for international students. In 2021, about 914,095 international students were pursuing their education in the United States, and 21,515 international students were in the state of Georgia (IIE, 2021). According to the CGE (2020) annual report, approximately 145 international students representing 47 countries were enrolled at UNG. Even though there has been some decrease in inbound international students coming to UNG in recent years due to the challenges of the pandemic and visa regulations, the CGE has developed a comprehensive international student enrollment management plan that seeks to increase the overall international student population to 345 by the end of the 2024–2025 academic year (UNG's International Student Recruitment Marketing Plan, 2021). This plan will develop innovative outreach opportunities for increasing international student population at UNG through multiple global partnership development and direct recruitment efforts.

Innovative International Student Recruitment

In the wake of COVID-19 pandemic and other geopolitical challenges, traditional international recruitment models have been challenged. CGE leadership, in turn, has reprioritized their efforts toward meaningful and sustainable international recruitment. According to the aforementioned ACE Internationalization Laboratory report, previous international recruitment efforts at UNG had mostly been led through various departments, such as the Center for Language Education, the Institute for Leadership and Strategic Studies, the Japanese language program, athletics, and undergraduate admissions (CGE, 2021). However, CGE, through its newly developed international student recruitment marketing plan, is looking to engage in innovative marketing initiatives in specific international student origin markets. These initiatives include digital marketing, working with education agents, virtual fairs, visiting high schools, peer-to-peer connections, and a detailed communications plan to reach prospective international student populations.

International Student Outreach

While the pandemic has presented several challenges for international education in terms of travel, UNG, under CGE's leadership, has developed several digital outreach and marketing efforts to connect with prospective international students. Martel (2021) has highlighted that out of 864 U.S. higher education institutions, 56% were involved in online recruitment events and approximately 55% utilized their social media platforms for student outreach during the fall 2021 term. As part of its ongoing outreach efforts, CGE has established partnerships with global digital platforms to share information about UNG's academic programs and student life with international students. CGE has also participated in virtual international recruitment fairs, targeting students in Southeast Asia and Latin America. UNG, through its communications platform (SLATE), has also developed a comprehensive email campaign for prospective applicants who are interested in learning more about the institution.

Developing Outreach Opportunities in Georgia

One in 10 Georgia residents is an immigrant (American Immigration Council, 2018). Due to this rich state diversity, UNG has started to focus its international student outreach efforts to several secondary schools in Georgia. The CGE, working in collaboration with enrollment management, is developing marketing admissions information specific to the needs of immigrant students. Two advantages of recruiting students who are first-generation residents have been their (1) understanding of the U.S. higher education system and (2) local family support. UNG is also planning to develop relationships with several foreign consulates in the state of Georgia to explore educational partnerships.

Primary International Student Markets for UNG

Currently, the CGE along with enrollment management has decided to focus on four primary international student markets for their outreach efforts: Vietnam, Mexico, Brazil, and Japan. The decision to focus on these specific international student markets was based upon the current enrollment of international students, languages that are being taught at

UNG, the immigrant communities that are close to UNG, and the current strategic partnerships that are being established in those respective markets. According to the Open Doors 2021 report, there were 21,631 international students from Vietnam, 12,986 international students from Mexico, 11,785 international students from Japan, and 14,000 international students from Brazil studying in the United States (IIE, 2021).

Developing International Partnerships

As part of its student outreach and international partnership development, UNG is exploring collaborations with Education USA, a U.S. Department of State network of international student advising centers in more than 170 countries, and U.S. commercial services, part of the U.S. Department of Commerce's International Trade Administration that offers a range of international trade expertise. UNG is also planning to expand its international network through participation in conferences with education agents, that is, commissioned education consultants who work with higher education institutions and prospective international students in finding best-fit academic opportunities for studying abroad. These meetings will provide an opportunity to forge connections in different parts of the globe to spread awareness about the UNG brand and find international students who might be a strong fit for UNG.

Conclusion: A Shared Future through Internationalization

Although it is difficult to predict the future of internationalization, one certainty is that UNG will remain focused on expanding its internationalization efforts in a concerted manner. Shifting geo-political issues directly affect global student mobility, so as UNG grows its international student and education abroad enrollment, the institution cannot rely solely on student mobility to create an internationalized environment. By embedding global learning into curricular and co-curricular activities, all students will have direct access to opportunities to develop their global awareness and their cross-cultural competencies. No one office or unit can achieve the goals of internationalization and a global learning environment on its own, nor should it. It will be vitally important for UNG to create a systemized and collaborative approach to this work as the university continues to develop internationalization as a key element to its institutional culture.

References

ACE Internationalization Laboratory. (2021). University of North Georgia. https://ung.edu/global-engagement/_uploads/files/ace-izn-final-report_web_2021.pdf

American Immigration Council. (2018). Immigrants in Georgia. https://www.americanimmigrationcouncil.org/sites/default/files/research/immigrants_in_georgia.pdf

Center for Global Engagement [CGE]. (2020). 2020 Annual Report. https://ung.edu/global-engagement/_uploads/files/2020-cge-annual-report.pdf

Center for Global Engagement [CGE] (2021). *ACE Internationalization Lab final report*. University of North Georgia. https://ung.edu/global-engagement/_uploads/files/ace-izn-final-report_web_2021.pdf

Federal Student Aid. (2021). *2021–2022 Federal Student Aid handbook*. U.S. Department of Education. https://fsapartners.ed.gov/knowledge-center/fsa-handbook/2021-2022

Huang, Y. (2022). *Investigating student development of intercultural communication competence through collaborative online international learning* [Doctoral dissertation, University of North Georgia]. https://digitalcommons.northgeorgia.edu/

Institute of International Educational Exchange [IIE]. (2021). *Open Doors 2021*. https://www.iie.org/en/Research-and-Insights/Publications/Open-Doors-2021

Martel, M. (2021). *Fall 2021 international student enrollment snapshot*. Institute of International

Education. https://www.iie.org/Research-and-Insights/Publications/Fall-2021-International-Student-Enrollment-Snapshot

Office of Academic Affairs. (n.d.). *UNG Academic Terms & Definitions*. University of North Georgia. https://ung.edu/academic-affairs/academic-terms-and-definitions.php

SUNY COIL Center. (n.d.). *Welcome*. https://coil.suny.edu/

UNESCO Institute for Statistics. (2018). *Outbound internationally mobile students by host region.* http://data.uis.unesco.org/Index.aspx?queryid=172

UNG QEP Design and Implementation Committee. (n.d.). *UNG Quality Enhancement Plan: On time & on target.* University of North Georgia. https://ung.edu/qep/index.php

Inclusion Means Serving Our Students and Our Community

Bryan L. Dawson, Efren A. Velazquez, Rebecca Johnston, and Pablo Bueno Mendoza

Building a Multicultural University of North Georgia

As the University of North Georgia (UNG) celebrates its 150th anniversary, this chapter examines the building blocks for its future as a multicultural university. The Council for the Advancement of Standards in Higher Education (2012) for Multicultural Student Programs and Services observes that the development of services for students around their backgrounds is essential, stating such services "often [include] advocating for changing policies, practices, and attitudes of the campus and its students and employees that inhibit student confidence and success." These recommendations for action and support at the implementation level are further supported by current discussions taking place at the governing board level. The Association of Governing Boards of Universities and Colleges (2021) has recently identified three strategies for making colleges and universities more responsive to the needs of justice, equity, and inclusion on college campuses:

1. Developing and applying an equity lens in the board's governance structures;
2. Applying a justice, equity, and inclusion lens throughout the university; and
3. Contributing to social justice and equity in the communities where the institution is located.

To fully understand paths forward, the current status of student experiences at the university needs assessment. Additionally, an examination of how faculty develop the skills required to effectively serve our increasingly diverse student body is necessary. To wit, three components of this chapter address three foundational areas for institutional change: understanding regional demographics, developing trends analysis around campus climate, and training around multicultural competency.

Dr. Dawson's section examines how campus climate research will lay the foundation for future programmatic development. As one of the authors who analyzed the data of the first campus climate study (the UCLA Diverse Learning Environments study) and a current member of the UNG Campus Climate workgroup, his insights into the development of UNG culture will inform policy decisions for the foreseeable future.

Dr. Velazquez's section shares the research he has conducted with Latinx student population growth. As noted in the Council for the Advancement of Standards in Higher Education, Latinx college-age students graduate at lower rates than their white peers (CAS, 2012). Essential to increasing this rate is the establishment of programs and services to address their functional needs in Predominantly White Institutions.

Dr. Johnston's section explains the current structure for the Center for Teaching, Learning, and Leadership. As a member of the Engaging Difficult Dialogues facilitation team and the primary investigator of a study into faculty development's role in building cross-culturally competent practitioners, her insights demonstrate the importance of training in preparing our campus for the changing demographics in the North Georgia region.

Using Research to Inform Multicultural Development at UNG

In the spring semester of 2015, the UNG Professional and Continuing Education catalog cover appeared in the mailboxes of families across the state and was quickly met with derision and outrage. The cover depicted two white men in suits outrunning a woman and a Black man in a track race, seemingly serving as a tone-deaf exemplar of white privilege and the subordination of women and minorities. News media articles quickly picked up the story, citing the image as offensive and questioning how an image could pass so many checks before being sent out.

As a response, UNG decided to employ a nationally normed climate assessment analysis, and, in the fall of 2016, the Diverse Learning Environments (DLE) survey was administered to students electronically across five campuses by the Higher Education Research Institute (HERI) at the University of California, Los Angeles (UCLA) in an administrative effort to determine the quality of—and potential issues with—UNG's diversity climate. The DLE measures students' perceptions regarding institutional climate, institutional diversity, individual social identity, intergroup relations, prevalence and experience of harassment, discrimination, and student learning outcomes. HERI provided the raw data to analysts at UNG, who provided the institution with information regarding student experiences at our five campuses. In the fall of 2021, the DLE survey was once again administered, along with the staff and faculty climate surveys, to capture the experiences of the entire university.

Collecting Data Longitudinally

Data gathered from institution-wide surveys allow us to capture the thoughts and voices of our faculty, staff, and student body. These data, in turn, enable administration to identify critical areas for consideration and improvement. Data presented by Dawson and Cuevas (2019), based on the initial DLE assessment, indicate that students who perceived that their institution was less open to diversity were more likely to desire to leave the institution. Moreover, this trend existed across students of all racial and ethnic backgrounds. Institutional data allows us to determine, at the macro level, the perception of representation, support, and the effectiveness of our programming across student groups. These data allow administration to understand the sub-climates (belonging, inclusion, and support) present within the institution and the perception of procedural and distributive justice for the members of the institutional community. By collecting the data over a longitudinal period, we can assess the impact of changes and make informed choices regarding where to redirect resources and where to leverage pillars of inclusiveness to build stronger programs that demonstrate a positive impact.

Using Data to Inform Future UNG Efforts

While larger climate assessment data is important, we also capture information at the programmatic level and use that information in conjunction with the macro data to make informed decisions yearly. For instance, we can identify the impact of key initiatives, such as the African American Male Initiative, on retention of students through the analysis of student-centered survey measures and formative assessment of the students engaged. In addition, data collected from the original 2016 DLE survey were instrumental in the development of the need for a $1.2 million Department of Education Grant, which established the McNair Scholars Program at UNG. The UNG McNair Scholars program, aimed at preparing students from marginalized backgrounds for doctoral study, collects formative and summative assessment information from its undergraduate students throughout the academic year, including their experiences on campus, their feedback on diversity initiatives and programming efforts, and their perceptions of academic support from the many departments on campus. These pieces of data, taken together with larger samples of students, allow us to effectively demonstrate the positive changes on students at the university. Moreover, the UNG McNair Scholars program has served over 60 first-generation, low-income, and ethnic minority students who have entered into masters and doctoral study due to the program's efforts.

Data collected but left unshared stifles development. Therefore, the University Diversity Action Committee is committed to communicating the results of climate assessment data with divisions such as student affairs, Staff and Faculty Diversity Council, the Provost's office, and the Faculty Senate. Moreover, partnering with these organizations allows us to answer timely challenges presented by each entity, present informed plans for changes to the institutional structure, and engage change levers at the upper levels. Beyond these impacts on the institution, we can make our data public. For example, we can inform the admissions office of the potential challenges incoming students are voicing, allowing these offices to anticipate the needs and concerns of students and their families when they choose to enroll at UNG. These efforts will allow us to address and serve our growing populations of color and marginalized groups at UNG, such as our Latinx student population.

The Latinx Student Population and Community

The state of Georgia's demographics have changed over the past 20 years. A thorough understanding of demographic changes on all five of the UNG campuses is vital to properly serve our student body. In particular, we have seen an increase of Latinx students enrolling since 2014, shortly after the consolidation of North Georgia College & State University and Gainesville State College. For example, in fall 2014, UNG reported that 879 Hispanic students were enrolled. These numbers began to exponentially grow in subsequent years (refer to Table 13.1), a change which reflects demographic shifts in the state of Georgia. Specifically, the Latinx population grew from 5.3% (approximately 400 thousand) to 8.8% (approximately 850 thousand) from 2000 to 2010 (U.S. Census Bureau, n.d.). Currently, it is estimated that 9.9% of Georgia's population identifies as Latinx or Hispanic (U.S. Census Bureau, 2021). As Georgia demographics shift, so will the students UNG recruits and serves in the future. For example, approximately 41.3% of the population in Hall County, where the UNG Gainesville is located, identify as Latinx (Hispanic Alliance GA, n.d.).

Table 13.1: Hispanic/Latinx Growth at UNG		
Semester	**Number of Hispanic/ Latinx Students**	**Percentage of Hispanic/ Latinx Students**
Fall 2015	1,667	9.6%
Fall 2016	2,085	11.4%
Fall 2017	2,323	12.4%
Fall 2018	2,629	13.3%
Fall 2019	2,748	13.9%
Fall 2020	2,884	14.6%
Fall 2021	2,872	15.1%

Between 2019 and 2021, two McNair Scholars completed two studies examining the reasons Latinx students enroll and perform well at UNG. Below is a summary of both studies:

Study One

The first study was conducted during the summer of 2019 and focused on the reasons current and former Latinx students enrolled at UNG. A sample of 34 participants answered the items assessing Latinx enrollment (M = 22.29, SD = 3.01), with 58.8% currently enrolled at UNG. Results showed common themes among those who responded to the item, "What are the main reasons you decided to enroll at UNG?" Some of the more common responses were (A) Affordability, (B) UNG is close to their home, and (C) The College Assistance Migrant Program (CAMP).

Study Two

The second study was conducted between summer 2020 and spring 2021 and focused on (A) What motivates Latinx students to perform well in college and (B) What UNG can do better to help them succeed. A sample of 114 undergraduate Latinx students (M = 20.46, SD = 2.88) completed a survey, with most identifying as female (67.5%) and as first-generation college students (64.9%). Students responded that their family (e.g., parents, sibling, and family's future) and self-goals (e.g., finding stability, being a role model, representing their culture, and focusing on their future self) were their biggest motivations to help them perform well in college. For the second question, common themes regarding what UNG can do to assist Latinx students consisted of (A) Having more Latinx representation and (B) More tools and resources for Latinx success.

Supporting UNG Latinx Students and the Local Community

Overall, these studies show how UNG is an important place for Latinx college students to participate in higher education. However, students believe that further resources can be provided to increase their success and graduate with a college degree. This perception is important to note, as only 24% of Latinx adults have a college degree, compared to 46% of White non-Latinos (Fain, 2020). Furthermore, as the Latinx community is growing around Hall County and surrounding areas, it would be important for UNG to establish strong relationships for future recruitment and to increase student success.

Currently, UNG has programs and scholarships that assist Latinx students. For example, one of the critical programs that promote Latinx student success is CAMP, which was renewed for $2.1 million for the 2020–2025 cycle. The CAMP program has worked with Latinx first-year students since 2015 by helping them adapt to college. This is done by providing them with resources such as peer mentoring, tutoring, and workshops throughout the academic year. UNG also has the Goizueta Foundation Scholarship that assists Latinx heritage students with financial need. The scholarship is under the Office of Multicultural Student Affairs and supervised by the Latino Student Success Coordinator. Finally, UNG has been a recipient of the Institute for Mexicans Abroad Becas Grant since 2020. The Becas Grant assists college students of Mexican descent by providing them with a scholarship at the start of the school year. UNG will continue to apply for this grant through a collaborative effort between Enrollment Management, Multicultural Student Affairs, and Latinx faculty/staff within the university, to continue assisting Mexican-descent college students.

Given the growing population of Latinx students enrolled at UNG, future avenues to increase student success are important to identify and consider. For example, once the Latinx student enrollment reaches 25%, UNG will be eligible to apply for Hispanic-Serving Institution (HSI) status. This status will allow the institution to receive grant money, provided by the U.S. Department of Education, to increase Latinx student success. Finally, it would be important to collaborate with local Latinx organizations (e.g., Hispanic Alliance GA and the Hispanic Organization Promoting Education) to reach out to the local Latinx community. Establishing a presence within the Latinx community will create a relationship between the institution and local organizations that may be beneficial in the long term, especially if UNG desires to become an HSI. In addition, these collaborations will provide service opportunities for both faculty and staff, which can be seen through events like *Café con Leche*, where the local Latinx community benefits by learning about the college experience and the resources UNG can provide. Beyond community engagement, the development of faculty capability, understanding, and comfort with diversity and inclusion is paramount.

Faculty Development at the University of North Georgia

The goal of most faculty development centers is "to build a productive culture of teaching and learning within an institution to maximize the ability of faculty to learn and students to learn" (Condon et al., 2016, p. 129). This interaction lies at the heart of institutions of higher education. Within the Office of the Provost, the Center for Teaching, Learning, and Leadership (CTLL) at UNG provides faculty development for the university across its five campuses in an effort to support the university's mission to provide a "student-focused environment that includes quality education, service, research and creativity" (UNG, 2021), and implicit in this charge is CTLL's focus on providing programming that cultivates diversity, equity, and inclusion for the university community as a whole. CTLL supports UNG's commitment to academic excellence and seeks to foster a community of scholar-teachers as they pursue research-based pedagogies and the implementation of effective and significant educational experiences. By doing so, the unit strives to impact not only faculty and teaching staff but also the educational environment our university's students experience.

As noted in Chapter 10, *Serving Students by Serving Faculty: The Beginnings and Futures of UNG's Center for Teaching, Learning, and Leadership* (Rifenburg & Runquist, 2023), CTLL is administered by a team of leaders, including a director, an associate director, two assistant directors, an office administrator and communications specialist, a team of six faculty fellows (including two senior fellows), eight academy directors and faculty mentors, and a managing editor of *Teaching Academic* (an online blog and scholarly teaching resource). CTLL organizes and facilitates multiple academies and series within four primary domains: academic leadership, career milestones, scholarly productivity, and teaching and learning. In addition, CTLL collaborates with other units to provide training, including the Difficult Dialogues Workshop, a workshop that is currently in its second iteration and seeks to support the university's efforts to provide Diversity, Equity, and Inclusion programming.

Within the domain of academic leadership, the unit provides programming for new chairs in the form of the New Chairs Workshop Series, administers university-wide internal awards, and facilitates external awards processes. Upon survey to individuals who participated in programming, 94% of respondents (*n* = 34) indicated that academic leadership training was "Very Effective" or "Effective" in developing leadership skills. Within the domain of career milestones, CTLL hosts New Faculty Orientation, provides a Community of Practice for newer faculty in the form of the New Faculty Institute, facilitates mentoring of incoming faculty and teaching staff within departments and units, and works in collaboration with Distance Education and Technology Integration to provide tenure and promotion workshops. Within the domain of scholarly productivity, CTLL facilitates the Faculty Academy on the Scholarship of Teaching and Learning, as well as programs designed to support scholarly productivity, including the Write Now Academy, Shut Up and Write, and Start Your Summer off "Write!" The unit also supports academic departments in organizing faculty writing group programs.

Within the domain of teaching and learning, CTLL facilitates the University System of Georgia's Chancellor's Learning Scholars program, the Faculty Academy on High Impact Education Practices, the Research-Based Teaching Program, the Teaching Conversations workshop series, the Scholarship of Teaching and Learning Academy, and the Writing Across the Curriculum program. Efforts to enhance faculty and teaching staff efficacy in all domains with which they engage and to systematically assess the impact of programming are essential to meet the changing needs of learners at UNG. CTLL yearly analyzes internal assessment data in addition to conducting needs assessments and surveys designed to assist the unit in providing programming faculty and teaching staff feel is most needed. In the most recent assessment report, 93% of respondents (*n* = 100) who participated in CTLL programming indicated that the usefulness of the programming was either "Very Good" or "Good."

Finally, it is noteworthy that, along with the university at large, CTLL had to move all programming to a virtual format with the advent of the global COVID pandemic. The unit was instrumental in collating resources for faculty and teaching staff who suddenly had to transition instruction online, and it successfully navigated the conversion of programming that had previously been fully synchronous and in-person to alternate formats.

In the unit's current needs assessment, 66% (n = 373) of respondents indicated that during non-pandemic times, the preferred method of delivery of faculty development content was either through a synchronous webinar, asynchronous content, or a fully online course. This data speaks to the effectiveness of CTLL's ability to transition online with the advent of the pandemic, and the unit will continue to provide a combination of both in-person and remote programming.

Conclusion

Collection of data about UNG student experiences is just beginning. As the university moves forward, the Office of Institutional Excellence (OIE) and the Office of Diversity and Inclusion (ODI) will be partnering with faculty to assess how the students perceive their environment. The research and analysis by faculty will provide guidance to the administration for the development of programs and services. These crucial pieces of information will be necessary to inform the work of CTLL in training our young and experienced faculty so they may better serve our increasingly diverse populations in an inclusive and knowledgeable manner. In addition, the collection of information regarding faculty and staff perceptions of university climate will establish the groundwork to better support marginalized members serving in these areas. The work of CTLL, OIE, and ODI will be instrumental in recruiting and retaining diverse faculty and staff.

The UNG Faculty Senate Diversity Council has noted that the collection of student experiential data will help provide direction for faculty training and advocacy for policy change. Based upon interaction with students over the last few years, this body has recommended to administration two new policies: (1) a resolution on inclusivity language for the supplemental syllabus and (2) gender inclusive housing. These advocacy efforts demonstrate how training faculty on cross-cultural competence can be incorporated into the curriculum and can have an impact of supporting students.

References

Association of Governing Boards of Universities and Colleges. (2021). *AGB board of directors' statement on justice, equity, and inclusion and guidance for implementation.* https://agb.org/agb-statements/agb-board-of-directors-statement-on-justice-equity-and-inclusion-and-guidance-for-implementation/

Council for the Advancement of Standards in Higher Education. (2012). *Multicultural student programs and services self-assessment guide.* https://www.cas.edu/store_product.asp?prodid=67

Condon, W., Iverson, E. R., Manduca, C. A., Rutz, C., & Willett, G. (2016). *Faculty development and student learning: Assessing the connections.* Indiana University Press.

Dawson, B. L., & Cuevas, J. (2019). An assessment of intergroup dynamics at a multi-campus university: One university, two cultures. *Studies in Higher Education, 45*(6), 1047–1063. https://doi.org/10.1080/03075079.2019.1628198

Fain, P. (2020, August 12) *Latinos' degree completion increases; Equity gaps remain.* Inside Higher Ed. https://www.insidehighered.com/quicktakes/2020/08/12/latinos-degree-completion-increases-equity-gaps-remain

Hispanic Alliance GA. (n.d.). *About us.* https://hispanicalliancega.org/about-us

U.S. Census Bureau. (n.d.). *2010 Georgia census data.* https://www.ncsl.org/documents/redistricting/georgia_census_data_2010.pdf

U.S. Census Bureau. (2021, July 1). *QuickFacts: Georgia.* https://www.census.gov/quickfacts/GA

University of North Georgia. (n.d.). *Mission, vision & values.* https://ung.edu/about/mission-vision-values.php

.

Glows and Grows of Promoting Allyship for Marginalized Populations through Organized Multicultural Structures

Winnifred Namatovu, Olivier Le Blond, and Pablo Bueno Mendoza

Introduction: A UNG History Primer

On this 150th anniversary of the University of North Georgia (UNG), it is necessary to see all multicultural/diversity efforts in light of the institution's history. As noted in Chapter 1, *A Brief History of the University of North Georgia* (Galloup, 2023), the original campus in Dahlonega was founded as a segregated institution during the Southern Reconstruction. Until the late 1950s, the Dahlonega Campus maintained a policy of segregation. William Pittman Roberts, in his *Georgia's Best Kept Secret: A History of North Georgia College*, documents the state policy on segregation. In 1959, two African Americans were admitted to North Georgia College (the present-day Dahlonega Campus).

After NGC was desegregated in 1959, Roberts noted that the Corps of Cadets was not desegregated until 1967:

> The first black, Kenneth Rouse, was admitted in 1965. After that, a few other blacks were admitted. By 1967, integration had come to be accepted as a matter of course, and there was never a real problem at NGC. Sometimes cade [*sic.*] officers from south Georgia gave the Blacks a little trouble, and sometimes they were roughed up on the football field. (pp. 104–105)

This short paragraph shows that some of the students at UNG did not fully accept desegregation. The Roberts history presents an administrative perspective that generally glosses over the experience of students. The African American students in the Corps of Cadets at that time were not interviewed concerning the treatment they received from their peers.

Gainesville Junior College's history is shorter, as the campus was founded during the large demographic growth in college-age students during the 1960s. Hence, the campus was integrated at its founding in 1964. The key thing to note about the historical legacy of this campus is its venerable support for the working class in Hall County. Other historical factors currently represent the campus's being integrated from its beginning; prior to consolidation in 2012, Gainesville State College was close to receiving the Hispanic-Serving Institution federal designation. As Dawson and Cuevas (2020) have noted, the Gainesville Campus's embrace of diversity is one of its distinguishing features.

UNG is a place where the state's changing demographics, particularly the northeast Atlanta Metro area, are becoming increasingly diverse due to immigrant relocations. Therefore, this chapter considers how institutional change can be leveraged to better support marginalized populations at UNG over the next 50 years. In the first section, Winnifred Namatovu and Olivier Le Blond examine the literature of multicultural structures and ally development within university communities in the United States. In the second section, they address these topics in reference to UNG. How is the academic side of UNG developing intentional diversity and inclusion? Namatovu is the lead for the College of Education's Diversity and Recruitment plan, which is the response to the Council for the Accreditation of Educator Preparation. She shares components of the unpublished UNG Diversity Action Plan that will be revisited now that the 2022–2027 Strategic Plan has received cabinet approval. Le Blond will look at the efforts marginalized communities at UNG made to improve the university environment. He will also examine how the campuses meet these populations' needs. In the third section, the authors offer hopes for expanding multiculturalism and allyship efforts at UNG.

Multiculturalism and Allyship in American Higher Education

What Is a Multicultural Structure and Why Does It Matter?

Although college campuses have continued to diversify over the past 50 years, some individuals continue to be marginalized by policies and practices within higher education institutions (Pope et al., 2014; U.S. Department of Education, 2016). To address this issue, many institutions have attempted to develop and implement initiatives that support the diverse experiences of their students. However, the current systems in place across colleges and universities in the United States continue to fail in supporting some of the following groups: students of color, students from socioeconomically disadvantaged backgrounds, students who are members of the LGBTQIA+ community, and students from minority religious organizations.

According to Pope et al. (2014), the reason for the lack of institutional success is because the efforts have been "sporadic, fragmented, and uncoordinated" (pp. 18–19). For that reason, they offer the framework of multicultural organization development (MCOD) as a tool for creating multicultural structures that are authentic, comprehensive, and sustainable.

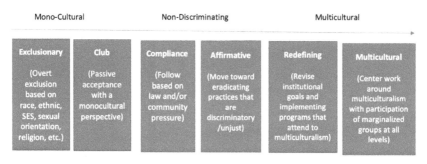

Figure 14.1: Modified from Jackson (2005) & Pope et al. (2014)

To create an effective multicultural structure, the following must be present: diverse knowledge and perspectives of members that shape the organization's work (e.g., mission, values, policies, practices, procedures) and equitable treatment of all members within the organization (Holvino, 2008). Such a process requires an organization to "fully embrace social justice before focusing on the structural diversity or numerical diversity of an organization" (Pope et al., 2014, p. 22). The attainment of social justice initiatives mandates a commitment to confronting exclusionary practices that promote racism, xenophobia, sexism, heterosexism, and religious oppression.

What is Allyship and Why Does it Matter?

Over the past few years, uses of the term *allyship* emerged when matters of diversity rose to the forefront of the media. However, what is allyship? Merriam Webster (n.d.) defines allyship as "the state or condition of being an ally; supportive association with another person or group" and specifies the following: "such association with the members of a marginalized or mistreated group to which one does not belong." Higher education institutions have often professed an interest in the well-being of marginalized students, faculty, and staff. And yet, there seems to be a disconnect between what institutions currently do to promote allyship and the needs of these marginalized populations.

American universities are a microcosm of the diversity present in the United States, and all races, religious beliefs, sexual orientations, genders, and identities are present on almost all U.S. campuses. Yet some marginalized students, faculty, and staff do not see themselves represented on their campuses. Representation matters; seeing oneself represented on campus has incommensurable value for students belonging to minoritized groups, whether they identify with racial, sexual, or gender minoritized populations. The first step in being an ally is to recognize that multiple factors come into play when a student belongs to a minoritized group. This calls on the notion of intersectionality, as defined by Kimberlé Crenshaw (1989). Simply put, intersectionality recognizes that multiple factors come into play when it comes to discrimination and privilege. Being an ally means recognizing the privileges one has; privileges come in many forms, such as race, social status, level of education, and immigration status. Being aware of one's own privileges also means being aware of the different types of oppression at stake when someone belongs to a marginalized community.

How have institutions addressed the issues facing marginalized students? National programs such as the Ronald E. McNair post-baccalaureate achievement program, created by the U.S. Department of Education, have expanded to more colleges than ever before. Additionally, cultural centers catering to a specific type of marginalized population have been created on campuses throughout the U.S., and curricula dealing with these populations in mind are designed to attract students to colleges. Human resources departments design trainings to teach faculty and staff the intricacies of issues faced by marginalized campus populations. These trainings help better identify the inequities that can affect students and their work in the faculty's courses (Haynie, 2018). A deeper understanding of these inequities is the crux that will allow faculty and staff to be better allies to our marginalized students.

Over the past decade, UNG has worked to integrate diversity, equity, and inclusion in its strategic plans, and as we celebrate the sesquicentennial anniversary of the institution, let us look at what UNG has accomplished to support its marginalized students.

Multiculturalism and Allyship at the University of North Georgia

Developing Multicultural Structures at UNG

Within UNG, the following steps have been taken to create a multicultural structure: the development of a Diversity Action Plan; the formation of Diversity, Equity, and Inclusion (DEI) committees in each college; and the creation of faculty/staff organizations for marginalized groups. During the 2020–2021 academic year, a committee of UNG faculty and staff was formed to develop a plan that would attend to diversity, equity, and inclusion issues while supplementing the goals of UNG's strategic plan. After multiple discussions, the committee identified areas of need and the following subcommittees were developed:

- Cross-Cultural Competencies and Curriculum
- Internal and External Relations Support Structures
- Outside Partnership and Relations
- Marginalized Populations and Specific Population Support
- Recruitment and Retention of Faculty and Staff
- Recruitment and Retention of Students

Although each subcommittee was tasked with developing recommendations unique to their area of focus, some similarities were apparent across the reports. The first recommendation was the implementation of a campus climate survey in order to gain insight into the experiences of faculty, staff, and students. The second recommendation was the creation of a university-wide coordinating committee that fosters and promotes the university's collective work on DEI efforts. The third recommendation was the implementation of university-wide, cross-cultural competence trainings for faculty and staff. The fourth recommendation was the addition of DEI efforts to faculty and staff expectations for promotion and/or tenure. The fifth recommendation was the development of equitable funding to support DEI initiatives across the university. The sixth recommendation was fostering partnerships across the university and surrounding communities that support DEI efforts resulting in long-term student development.

The Cross-Cultural Competencies and Curriculum subcommittee was tasked with developing recommendations for faculty and staff training that foster cross-cultural competence for high interaction with diverse student populations. To begin, the subcommittee looked at multiple definitions of cross-cultural competence. Next, the group examined critical elements for effectively promoting cross-cultural competence at every level of the institution. The definitions and critical elements informed the development of the following recommendations: integration of DEI efforts throughout the university's strategic plan and initiatives, an increase in advertising faculty and staff trainings focused on DEI, the creation of a platform that offers resources and professional development opportunities to UNG community members (e.g., faculty, staff, students, and community partners), the requirement of Safe Zone training for all faculty and staff, and active participation of human resources staff in DEI professional development workshops so that they can design and implement appropriate practices to support faculty and staff search committees.

The Internal and External Relations Support Structures subcommittee focused on civic engagement efforts to support faculty and the diverse student population on all five UNG campuses. They divided their final recommendations into three sections: (1) planning and recruitment, (2) assessments of civic engagement, and (3) intercampus civic engagement. Within the area of planning and recruitment, the subcommittee made the following recommendations: consistent meetings of a Civic Action Plan (CAP) Implementation Committee to set and monitor university-wide goals, involvement of the Office of Community Engagement and Regional Campus Leadership to identify potential external partners, and creation of workgroups focused on incorporating diversity and inclusion efforts into civic engagement initiatives within internal and external partnerships. In the area of assessments of civic engagement, the following actions were offered: creation of a plan that includes explicit goals and objectives to support civic engagement, selection and implementation of multiple methods to evaluate civic engagement efforts, and the use of assessment measures to provide purposeful feedback to faculty and students committed to engaging in meaningful civic engagement. For the area of intercampus civic engagement, the subcommittee suggested the development and implementation of opportunities for faculty, staff, and students from all five campuses to engage in community-engaged learning; support for faculty seeking intercampus collaboration and internal funding to develop and implement initiatives focusing on civic engagement; and the formation of projects with community organizations (near all five campuses) to support UNG's diverse population.

The Outside Partnership and Relations subcommittee was charged with compiling recommendations for strengthening partnerships with external organizations that currently, or could, support UNG's DEI efforts. In order to narrow down their recommendations, the subcommittee examined DEI demographics, attitudes, and initiatives at UNG, communities within UNG's 30-county service area, and USG's policies and procedures regarding DEI efforts. As a result, the group proposed seeking external funding to support recruitment efforts for underserved populations and civic engagement; providing opportunities to develop or expand faculty, staff, and student networks focused on DEI initiatives; and leading a regional event (e.g., conference or educational program) that promotes DEI efforts.

The Marginalized Populations and Specific Population Support subcommittee initially focused on identifying common principles and practices for creating an inclusive community at UNG. During their exploration, they identified the following issues: the term *multicultural* is complex, programming should be evidence- and data-driven, and intersectionality must be considered with program planning and implementation. In order to address their findings, they proposed the following recommendations: an assessment of UNG's current DEI issues across all campuses, the creation of a standing DEI council until a DEI-staffed center is established; the development and implementation of a process that actively advertises faculty and staff positions outside the usual outlets in order to attract a diverse pool of applicants; the inclusion of holidays from a variety of religious groups on UNG's calendar; the modification of names for student resources and services so that they are more inclusive (e.g., Disability Services to Student Accessibility Services); the development of a diversity book club for faculty, staff, and students; gender-neutral bathrooms in all buildings across all campuses and gender-neutral housing options; and ensuring that all curriculum materials include examples from diverse groups.

The Recruitment and Retention of Faculty and Staff subcommittee was charged with outlining recommendations to increase overall institutional diversity and inclusion of "minoritized" employees. Using multiple literature sources on best practices and general guides from other higher education institutions, the subcommittee developed recommendations targeting the following three areas: (1) reaching, recruiting, and retaining a talented pool of diverse workers; (2) the role of administrators in recruiting and retaining diverse employees; and (3) the UNG hiring process. For the first area, the group suggested making diversity part of the employment brand, casting a wider net to find a diverse pool of candidates, integrating diversity into talent management and succession planning, and letting employees take the lead with managing and programming efforts related to diversity issues. Within the second area, the group suggested the use of open searches, requiring all search committee members to participate in "Workforce Diversity Recruitment and Retention Best Practices" in addition to Affirmative Action/Equal Opportunity training, publicly recognizing departments/units that successfully increase diversity and excellence in their faculty and staff, providing new hiring resources to increase diversity, and establishing search committees that are diverse in demographics and expertise but homogeneous in their commitment to equitable hiring processes. In the third area, the group proposed amending policy 2.0 on hiring committee composition and selection to emphasize the importance of diversity representation on the search committees, developing and implementing a required search committee training on the process and importance of diversity considerations, and posting job opportunities in a variety of locations (e.g., social media, professional associations, networks promoting DEI efforts).

The Recruitment and Retention of Students subcommittee referred to UNG's vision for increasing access to higher education for historically underrepresented and economically disadvantaged populations as well as creating an inclusive environment that promotes success for all students. The group divided their recommendations into the following four sections: (1) staff, (2) scholarships, (3) messaging, and (4) support. For the first section, they recommended that the Office of Multicultural Student Affairs be provided with resources to support and expand upon their diversity initiatives (e.g., staff and funding). For the second section, they suggested that there should be an increase in scholarship and grant offerings by devoting more personnel to seek out funding opportunities. For the third section, they proposed ensuring that there are clear and consistent processes for messaging, especially during "volatile situations." Lastly, the group advised developing a plan for student clubs and organizations to promote campus diversity and/or offer diverse student populations avenues for social connectedness. Additionally, the group advocated for implementing a process to regularly evaluate gaps in representation and potential barriers that need to be addressed (e.g., eligibility, application and admissions, access and financing, community college pathways, and college transitions).

Developing Allies at UNG

In terms of developing allies for our marginalized students, UNG has worked to implement several entities and/or support programs designed to bring awareness to the inequities that exist for our marginalized students. Such examples are the creation of the Office of Multicultural Student Affairs, training programs such as Green Zone and Safe Zone, and the creation of the Office of Diversity and Inclusion. While the Office of Diversity and Inclusion is an essential addition to UNG's social fabric, the first three entities will be looked at in greater detail over the following few paragraphs.

Prior to the consolidation and creation of UNG, the Office of Multicultural Student Affairs (MSA) existed as separate entities on the two larger campuses. Since its creation as a consolidated entity, MSA is present on three campuses (Dahlonega, Gainesville, and Oconee) and has been instrumental in the promotion and well-being of marginalized students. The MSA staff serve as advisors of several student clubs that cater to marginalized students: LSA/LASO (Latino Student Association/Latin American Student Organization), BSU (Black Student Union), Spectrum/GSA (LGBTQIA+ student organizations), and ASA (Asian Student Association). These student clubs contribute to the visibility of UNG's marginalized student population through the events they hold every semester. They are instrumental in the recruitment of future students coming from marginalized backgrounds. If prospective students see themselves represented, they will be more likely to consider UNG as their university of choice. MSA does not just advise student clubs; the office hosts two scholarships that help support minoritized student populations: the Goizueta Foundation Scholarship supports Latinx students, and the Mattie Moon Foundation Scholarship supports African American students. These scholarships are awarded to help students in financial need as long as they meet certain criteria, one of them being their racial identification. The MSA Office is also responsible for bringing awareness during celebratory months, such as Black History Month, Hispanic Heritage Month, AAPI Heritage Month, Women's History Month, or Native American Heritage Month. During these celebratory months, speakers, events, and film screenings are organized for the entire campus population. These events are a way to educate the student body, but all of them are open to faculty, staff, and the community at large. Through these events, the multicultural aspects of UNG have greater visibility to the entire college community.

The Green Zone and Safe Zone programs are trainings designed to educate the campus body about the needs and specificities of two specific student populations: veterans and LGBTQIA+ students. UNG prides itself on being one of the six senior military colleges in the country. Its veteran student population is significant, and this specific population has needs that differ from other students. Green Zone intends "to empower UNG faculty and staff to support student veterans as they transition from military life to a college environment" (NEST, n.d.). Created in 2010 by Ann Nichols-Casebolt at Virginia Commonwealth University, the program makes sure that volunteers "have basic knowledge of the challenges faced by student veterans, as well as information about the resources available on campus and in the community to assist them" (Nichols-Casebolt, 2012, p. 27). Nichols-Casebolt modeled the Green Zone program on the Safe Zone program, another training opportunity offered at UNG.

Safe Zone is designed to educate participants on the complexities of sexual orientations and genders. While the program existed under different names pre-consolidation, it was revived through the MSA Office, but trainings were offered too sporadically. Several faculty and staff members expressed interest in being trained to lead training, and several became certified trainers in spring 2019. Since then, the program has been offered on a per-need basis, as all trainers volunteer their own time outside of their main duties. The program has been very successful, and many faculty and staff members have been trained since 2019. The existence of such a program is vital in the Northeast Georgia region due to the more conservative nature of the area and the proximity of the city of Atlanta, which has a significant homeless LGBTQIA+ youth population (Our House, 2016.).

Additionally, over the last few years, not only has the visibility of marginalized students increased on all of our UNG campuses but also the visibility of marginalized faculty members, who have created organizations to show support to other marginalized faculty and staff members. In the past two years, UNG has seen the creation of the following organizations: the Black Faculty/Staff Association, the Latinx Committee, a LGBTQ+ Organization, the Faculty Women of Color Teaching Circle, and the Women's Leadership/Network. While all these programs and organizations are important, worthy of celebration, and integral to the creation of a population of allies on all UNG campuses for our marginalized students, it is important to look toward the future and expand the visibility of allies at UNG.

Moving Forward: What Should Multiculturalism and Allyship at UNG Look Like in the Future?

The Future of Multicultural Structures for UNG

While having made positive strides toward creating multicultural structures that improve the experiences of faculty, staff, and students, UNG still has opportunities for growth. Pope et al. (2014) note that the development of successful multicultural structures does not occur through "an immediate and short-term process" (p. 30); it takes time and effort. They add that continuous reexamination of the group's "mission, objectives, policies, procedures, and practices" (p. 30) must take place, especially when new members join the group. As UNG works to recruit and retain more diverse faculty, staff, and students, university-wide efforts must be put forth to evaluate and modify our current systems so that real and meaningful change can take place.

The Future of Allyship for UNG

One step to undertake in the creation of a culture of allyship at UNG is the creation of counterspaces. These spaces are "physical locations within an existing environment that are affirming as well as comfortable niches of interactions that can be verbal or nonverbal, for marginalized or oppressed groups" (Howard-Hamilton & Hinton, 2016, p. 30). These spaces may be physical (such as cultural centers) or community-based (e.g., students of a marginalized group gathering together in a classroom or cafeteria). Examples of counterspaces that could exist at UNG are a LGBTQ+ Center or a Hispanic Studies Center. Additionally, the recruitment and retention of equity-minded faculty will increase not only the visibility of allies on UNG campuses but also diversity at the institution. The hiring of such individuals will, in turn, allow for the creation of curricula targeted to these marginalized students. Courses rooted in Chicano/a studies, LGBTQ+ studies, and

African American/Black studies will show marginalized students that they matter and are represented on campus.

While all six colleges present at UNG have, as of 2022, college-specific diversity councils, any Diversity, Equity, and Inclusion initiative—or any effort to support UNG's marginalized students—will be rendered void without institutional support. Institutional support can come in many shapes, not solely financial. Truly promoting and supporting marginalized students in a non-performative way means getting full support from the upper administrators at all levels (department heads, deans, associate VPs, and provosts). It also involves truly listening to the needs and concerns of our marginalized student population. If UNG strives to implement its values of excellence, student-focus, integrity, engagement, and service, institutional support for all of its marginalized students should be a priority. Only then will UNG truly attain its vision to become "a regional and national leader for academic excellence, engagement, educational opportunity, and leadership development" (UNG, n.d.).

References

Crenshaw, K. (1989). Demarginalizing the intersection of race and sex: A black feminist critique of antidiscrimination doctrine, feminist theory, and antiracist politics. *University of Chicago Legal Forum, 1989*(1), 139–167. https://doi.org/10.4324/9780429500480-5

Dawson, B. L., & Cuevas, J. A. (2020). An assessment of intergroup dynamics at a multi-campus university: One university, two cultures. *Studies in Higher Education, 45*(6), 1047–1063. https://doi.org/10.1080/03075079.2019.1628198

Haynie, A. (2018). Equity-minded faculty development. *To Improve the Academy: A Journal of Educational Development, 37*(1). https://doi.org/10.3998/tia.17063888.0037.107

Howard-Hamilton, M. F., & Hinton, K. G. (2011). Oppression and its effect on college student identity development. In M. J. Cuyjet, C. Linder, M. F. Howard-Hamilton, & D. L. Cooper (Eds.), *Multiculturalism on campus: Theory, models, and practices for understanding diversity and creating inclusion* (pp. 19–36). Stylus.

Merriam-Webster. (n.d.). Allyship. In *Merriam-Webster.com dictionary.* https://www.merriam-webster.com/dictiionary/allyship

Our House. (2016, October 2). *More than 3,300 youth are homeless in Atlanta area, project by Georgia State and Partners finds.* https://ourhousega.org/congressional-approval-of-education-platform/

Nichols-Casebolt, A. (2012). The green zone: A program to support military students on campus. *About Campus: Enriching the Student Learning Experience, 17*(1), 26–29. https://doi.org/10.1002/abc.21070

Nighthawk Engagement & Student Transitions [NEST]. (n.d.). *Green zone.* University of North Georgia. https://ung.edu/nest/veterans-military/green-zone.php

Pope, R. L., Reynolds, A. L., & Mueller, J. A. (2014). *Creating multicultural change on campus.* John Wiley & Sons.

Roberts, W. P. (1998). *Georgia's best kept secret: A history of North Georgia College.* North Georgia College Alumni Association.

U.S. Department of Education. (2016, November). *Advancing diversity and inclusion in higher education.* Office of Planning, Evaluation and Policy Development and Office of the Under Secretary. https://www2.ed.gov/rschstat/research/pubs/advancing-diversity-inclusion.pdf

Presidential Leadership of UNG: Building Partnerships to Advance the Success of Students and North Georgia Communities

Ariel Turner and Bonita Jacobs

North Georgia College & State University (NGCSU) was founded in 1873 as the Military College of Georgia and was designated as one of only six federally designated senior military colleges in the nation. However, it was announced in 2011 that the university would consolidate with Gainesville State College (GSC) to become the University of North Georgia (UNG). In addition to GSC and NGCSU, Gainesville had a second campus in Watkinsville (Oconee County), and the two institutions were in the process of adding a campus in Cumming (Forsyth County) that would establish a two-plus-two program, enabling students to earn both an associate's and bachelor's degree in four years. In December 2012, SACSCOC accredited the institution and its four campus locations. The University System of Georgia Board of Regents approved the consolidation in January 2013. In 2015, a fifth campus was added in Blue Ridge to create a five-campus regional university with approximately 20,000 students.

While retaining its senior military college designation, UNG is also designated by the University System of Georgia (USG) as a State Leadership Institution. Further, the university is classified by the Carnegie Foundation as a Community Engagement Institution. UNG offers students a unique educational experience with degree programs ranging from associate to doctoral degrees, with continued growth, particularly in producing baccalaureate and graduate degrees.

Dr. Bonita Jacobs took office as the 17th president of NGCSU in 2011 as UNG's first female president and only the second woman to lead one of the country's six senior military colleges. She presided over the consolidation of NGCSU and GSC. As of fall 2022, Dr. Jacobs has the longest tenure of all current USG presidents. Dr. Ariel Turner is an alumna of the UNG Higher Education Leadership and Practice doctoral program. Her dissertation research focused on the lived experiences of women presidents of higher education institutions within the boundaryless career framework. This essay presents a culmination of these two perspectives with special emphasis on the uniqueness of UNG, the relationship of the institution with the local community, and the core competencies needed to lead a growing multi-campus university with multiple pathways to graduation. Under Dr. Jacobs's leadership, UNG's vision for its future became the primary focal area in which to include student success initiatives leading to strong retention and graduation rates, and this essay also addresses the results of this vision and initiatives.

Leadership of Higher Education Institutions and UNG

Modern-Day Higher Education Leadership

Leading a modern-day higher education institution is a complex juggling act requiring a variety of skills and competencies. As Madsen (2008) notes, "higher education institutions must have leaders who are capable, strong, smart, strategic, ethical, honest, motivating, inspirational, competent, innovative, creative, networked, organized, empowering, perceptive, reflective, collaborative, and insightful" (p. 13) The university presidency is a challenging role due to not only the unique financial complexities of higher education as an industry in an era of increased student loan debt and decreased appropriations but also concurrent relationship-based challenges, including navigating complex relationships with faculty governance, governing boards, community partnerships, public opinion, and the media. Presidents play a unique role. On the one hand, they are expected to be presidential in all things; on the other hand, they also must be humble and approachable in order to build trust and stakeholder buy-in.

The authors identified crucial components of presidential leadership. First and foremost is the importance of understanding the academic mission of the institution and how to create a strong environment that enables student success. Understanding the academic mission ties directly into the need for institutional fit between a president and an institution. A strong president at one institution would not necessarily be a good fit at another. On a more pragmatic level, a president also must understand student needs, including an understanding of why students leave the institution or are not progressing to graduation.

Skills for Higher Education Leaders

Since communication is a critical skill with regard to their day-to-day internal work, a university president must also possess strong communication skills. Leaders must communicate to and with faculty, staff, students, alumni, and the community about what is happening and what is changing at their institution. When examining the lived experience of women presidents, communication was identified as a core skill, including communication style, messaging, listening, and public speaking (Turner, 2021). The skill of communication was an essential aspect of UNG's successful consolidation, a process that also required successful teambuilding across all four campuses. The involvement of campuses in consolidation also speaks to the importance of establishing trust for a leader of a higher education institution. Building a strong and capable team has been particularly relevant to UNG, as the honest and excellent advice of the president's cabinet over the years has been critical to the institution's success.

Related to the skills of communication and ability to establish trust is the characteristic of empathy in a leader. The consideration of empathy was especially consequential during the challenges of the COVID-19 pandemic. Presidents as leaders need to understand, and mitigate, difficulties for faculty, staff, and students, help students progress toward graduation, and ensure that an institution continue to function and move forward. When considering the various challenges of the pandemic, individual hardships and difficulties, and the constraints and challenges caused by abrupt changes in modality and impacts on higher education finance, the ability to empathize and understand various stakeholders proves essential for a leader. Serving as an empathetic leader is relevant pragmatically; presidents must understand that all students are equally important but may have different needs, so it is important that they consider and empathize with the different student experiences. The ability to empathize with varying student experiences is particularly important for a leader of a multi-campus institution who must put into place leadership on each campus and create a sense of belonging and empowerment for faculty, staff, and students on each one. According to recent research focused on the lived experience of women presidents, a president's ability to empathize with others can facilitate the development of relationships with stakeholders both internal and external to the institution, by incorporating varied perspectives (Turner, 2021). An empathetic perspective may also encourage transparency in communication and enhance a president's ability, when making decisions, to consider their potential impact on all stakeholders.

Fundraising, which at times is a component of relationships between an institution and the community, is also an important skill for modern-day higher education leaders. While some find fundraising distasteful, it is, at its core, a function of supporting students and the institution's success. If an institution can secure fundraising dollars for student scholarships, higher education becomes more accessible to those who might not have the financial means to either attend or continue to matriculate. Through scholarships, external grants, legislative support, and other initiatives, higher education institutions can significantly and positively impact the lives of students.

Leadership of UNG

Regarding UNG, in particular, and the experience of presiding over a consolidation, a leader must understand the institution well enough to recognize the particular strengths of the existing campuses and conceptualize areas for their growth and improvement, including recognizing that each campus possesses a unique set of traditions and cultures that need to be maintained in this growth. Important to UNG's culture is its distinct team-based spirit—a spirit reflected in their student leaders—along with a strong work ethic. The focus on teamwork, academic excellence, and character development are present in UNG's central values of excellence, student focus, integrity, engagement, and service (University of North Georgia, 2022). UNG's central values and culture may be attributed to a combination of both the military heritage of the Dahlonega Campus and the parallel focus on student success at the former GSC campuses. Some of UNG's culture could also be attributed to its region.

Although UNG has students from all 50 states, the culture of the North Georgia region is reflected in the institution's values. The strong element of student leadership that helps drive UNG's culture ties in with regional cultural characteristics. North Georgia culture values neighbors helping neighbors and generally taking care of one another. The resulting valuing of communal hospitality corresponds with UNG's team-based spirit. Considering the culture of the local community is critical to higher education institutions. Higher education institutions should strive to foster "town/gown" relationships between the community and the institution in order to promote the success of both, referring to the partnership between a community (town) and the local higher education institution (gown). Embracing the regional culture at some level within the institution can therefore help facilitate the community/institution relationship.

Institutional Impact

When reflecting on the skills needed for modern higher education leaders, how those skills impact an institution, and UNG's successes, it is evident that leadership at UNG has made a positive impact on the institution. Over the course of the last decade, UNG has become nationally competitive with scholarships, including being named a top producer for Fulbright awards five years in a row. UNG has also shown continuously evolving success with other scholarships, including Boren, Gilman, Jack Kent Cooke, Goldwater, Truman, and Pickering, among others. The downstream implications of such a strong showing in nationally competitive scholarships is in their direct and positive impact on North Georgia students, enabling more students to continue in their education despite financial challenges. The success of UNG students with regards to prestigious awards also speaks to the strong reputation the institution has built and the high caliber of its students.

The last several years have also brought positive retention and graduation rates and an increase in academic offerings. A dramatic increase in fundraising includes a substantial number of endowments supporting important institutional initiatives. Presidential Incentive Awards, for example, have fueled a significant increase in research. There has also been an increase in external grants awarded to UNG faculty. UNG has added significantly more graduate programs while also maintaining and enhancing the strength of its military program. In addition to these beneficial advancements over the past few years are future initiatives at UNG to capitalize on its momentum and growth, focused on continuing to partner with the local community in town/gown relationships for the betterment of the institution and the community.

Higher Education Leadership and Community Partnerships

Related to the importance of higher education leaders understanding the regional culture of an institution to facilitate relationship building is recognizing the broad geographic area of Georgia that UNG serves, in terms of educational opportunities, enrollment in higher education, and college completion rates. There is a strong interest in and need for providing higher education opportunities to the students in the North Georgia region. UNG therefore has taken the initiative of expanding into Blue Ridge to provide more opportunities for public higher education to students who did not previously have ease of access. The expansion into communities seeking higher education opportunities reflects the comprehensive regional university approach, emphasizing the importance of town/gown relationships as well as the seeking of opportunities for partnering with and supporting local communities.

Successful town/gown relationships require openness, transparency, and continued discussions about how one works with the other. According to Gavazzi (2008), "it is important to emphasize that town/gown relationships are not static, but rather reflect a dynamic process that evolves over time" (p. 18). Viewing the relationship between a community and the institution as dynamic helps to contextualize the importance of consistent communication, which again speaks to the benefit of strong communication skills for a higher education leader. Because it is important to the dynamic and evolving nature of town/gown relationships, patience becomes another important characteristic for leaders. A benefit to higher education presidents is their understanding that, regarding partnerships with the local community, a "no" today might just mean "not at this time." Patience and strong communication allow higher education leaders to develop relationships externally and to pursue partnerships at a time that benefits both the institution and local community.

UNG and the Future

UNG currently has campuses in five cities: Gainesville, Dahlonega, Cumming, Blue Ridge, and Watkinsville. The institution has developed plans to address infrastructure needs to accommodate growth for each of its campuses. Funding has been awarded that will more than double the size of the Blue Ridge Campus and enable additional degrees to address critical need areas for the region, including an emphasis on nursing and an expansion of lab capabilities. The institution will also emphasize further developing community relationships through creating available space to accommodate community events. In relatively small communities, a campus needs to feel a part of their community, and vice versa. With the focus of a town/gown relationship in Blue Ridge in mind, UNG therefore intends to welcome the community to campus for events in order to further immerse the community in terms of shared community space. With the growth of the Cumming Campus, UNG will also add considerable space to accommodate the increasing demand. As a result of a generous donation, in fall 2022 Dahlonega will open a new facility for the Mike Cottrell College of Business, and generous alumni support will also enable a new military complex for a growing Corps of Cadets program. The UNG Gainesville Campus has acquired and refurbished property adjacent to campus, thereby adding significantly to the available space for this rapidly growing community.

The infrastructure developments for UNG serve as a physical manifestation of the growth of the institution in the past 10 years and well represent the connections the institution has to the communities in North Georgia. When reflecting on the past 10 years of leadership at UNG and what the future holds for this institution, the sesquicentennial will be a timely celebration of a successful university that continues to grow both geographically and with regard to programs and partnerships.

References

Gavazzi, S. M. (2018). Campus and community leadership in the spotlight: How university presidents and city managers view town/gown relationships. *Journal of Community Engagement and Scholarship*, *11*(1), 8–19.

Madsen, S. R. (2008). *On becoming a woman leader: Learning from the experiences of university presidents*. Jossey-Bass.

Turner, A. (2021). *The lived experience of women presidents within the boundaryless career perspective* [Doctoral dissertation, University of North Georgia]. https://ir.ung.edu/work/sc/25a72082-01ac-4202-b82c-bfd84cfd058a

University of North Georgia. (2022). *Mission, vision & values*. https://ung.edu/about/mission-vision-values.php

Public Scholarship for Societal Engagement: Envisioning the Future of Research at Regional Universities

Michael Lanford

The Exhilaration of Research and the Limitations of Its Impact

From 2016 to 2017, I was living my dream in Florida. For most people visiting Florida, such a vision might entail frequent outings to the gorgeous array of beaches throughout the state; weekend trips to Busch Gardens, Harry Potter World, and the Magic Kingdom; firsthand encounters with alligators, dolphins, and manatees; and maybe a football game or two. For me, however, the "dream" involved daily visits to a college campus; weekend injections of caffeine in a less-than-stunning array of coffee shops; firsthand encounters with perplexed students, overworked professors, and frustrated college administrators; and some unrecorded moments where people from all ages and walks of life confided some of their deepest concerns and fears about their college coursework, their jobs, their relationships, and their futures.

I was writing my dissertation: a study of first-year writing classes at an open-access state college. The college was similar to many throughout each of our 50 states. It was a deeply underfunded institution where every budget announcement instigated a palpable sense of dread that made the humid Florida air almost impossible to inhale. On each of the five campuses, students hurried, often in full sprint, between classes while working multiple jobs, caring for their children and their elderly parents, and surviving under the national threshold for poverty. Staff who worked in the institution's libraries, financial aid offices, advising centers, athletic facilities, and food pantries for 20, 30, even 40 years were more than willing to share stories about their happiest moments in their jobs (usually involving a student who finished a degree despite overwhelming odds) and some of their deepest regrets (also usually concerning a student who either disappeared from campus or ran out of money to finish their degree). The picture I am painting of this institution may seem depressing, but it was filled with individuals from all walks of life who believed in the power of higher education to overcome significant social stratification and help students achieve a better life for themselves and their loved ones. From the state neglect of a proud public educational institution to the boundless optimism of its stakeholders, the college was a microcosm of U.S. society.

Therefore, I considered it a privilege to document the daily experiences of students as they attempted to navigate a college environment that was—despite the best intentions of professors and college staff—often alienating. Each weekday morning at 7:30 am, I arrived on one of the college's five campuses so I could attend a couple of classes, check in on a few students, and informally talk with staff in various campus offices. The afternoons were reserved for individual interviews with students, professors, and administrators as well as the review of my observational notes from the morning classes. By 6 pm, I would welcome many of the college's adult learners to campus, attend classes with them, and perhaps share a meal (or beer) after class with them. Such activities are common for "ethnographic research," where the researcher attempts to experience daily life in an environment in a manner as closely as possible to that of the research participants. From the standpoint of the researcher, one goal of ethnography is to develop strong bonds of trust with research participants so that they share their ideas and skepticism. In other words, the research participants are an essential critical voice—letting you know when your observations are misguided, your questions are naive, or your conclusions are divorced from reality. I generally love it when participants not only question my research findings but also challenge me on core beliefs that might prevent greater self-reflection and realization.

During the final week of the fall 2016 semester, however, I was taken aback for a moment by a focus group conversation with seven students in a first-year writing class. I had gotten to know the students quite well because I attended 16 classes with them from September to November. Each of them knew probably as much about me as I knew about them. Thus, it wasn't surprising when an intrepid 35-year-old woman we will call Terra suddenly turned to me and said, "Something's been on our minds, Michael, and I hope you don't mind if we ask you a question."

Before I even had an opportunity to respond with a "Sure" or a "Go ahead," Terra continued.

"So, you've been recording us and taking notes for four months, and you're going to write this long dissertation—it sounds like hell—that makes you a doctor. That's great, but um, like who reads this? And when do things change?"

I would love to say that I had an adequate answer for Terra. I wanted to believe that my dissertation would be instantly read by influential policymakers, powerful business people, college trustees, and numerous other stakeholders who care deeply about the impact of higher education on state prosperity and the intellectual vitality of their local communities. Most importantly, I wanted to assure Terra and her classmates that the valuable time they spent with me would result in immediate change that could have a positive impact on their own college trajectories and their lives. But to say so would have been a lie. I was a fledgling doctoral student who was unlikely to find a broad audience with a doctoral dissertation, even though I had accumulated hundreds of hours of recordings, thousands of pages of transcriptions, and had actionable findings on an array of topics from support for first-generation students to the role of performance funding. I eventually published articles and book chapters that use dissertation data from students like Terra (e.g., Lanford, 2019, 2020, 2021b), as well as a book on innovation in higher education with my doctoral advisor that was deeply informed by my dissertation (Lanford & Tierney, 2022). And yet, I imagine those articles and book chapters have mostly circulated in scholarly circles. Sadly, Terra, I am still not quite sure when things will change.

Outlining a Public Scholarship Agenda for the University of North Georgia

Nevertheless, this chapter is an attempt to address Terra's questions by articulating a scholarly agenda for the University of North Georgia

(UNG) that could reflect its institutional aspirations; its vast potential for institutional growth, particularly in master's and doctoral programs; and its unique status as the leadership college for the University System of Georgia. My goals in this chapter are twofold. First, I will underscore the importance of public scholarship at a university like UNG, which has a compact to serve regional needs and stakeholders and cultivate community partnerships (Pearl, 2023). In this chapter, I define public scholarship as any writing that deliberately attempts to convey the findings, implications, and societal importance of university-sponsored research to local communities. Public scholarship traditionally has been published in newspapers, magazines, and other public-facing print periodicals, but it is increasingly produced through blogs, social media services like Twitter, websites sponsored by private foundations, and other forms of digital media. My justification for this stance on public scholarship reflects two contemporary concerns: (1) an amplified and (in my opinion) justified mandate for public accountability in higher education and (2) the increased likelihood that empirically sound research will be disregarded by the public because of a perceived lack of researcher credibility. I will return to these two issues—public accountability and researcher credibility—throughout the chapter.

Second, I assume a cautionary stance by outlining the very real and imminent barriers to public scholarship at UNG. These barriers include (1) a lack of training opportunities for doctoral students and early-career professors to participate in public scholarship and community outreach; (2) institutional mission creep, in which colleges and universities vie for prestige as defined by a limited set of metrics that are generally defined by elite institutions and neglect public engagement; and (3) contemporary threats to academic freedom and tenure that will, if left unchecked, create an environment of self-censorship where scientific experts are cowered into silence and the conditions for innovation and regional growth will suffer. Through the citation of examples from other colleges and universities—as well as my own personal experiences researching higher education in disparate locations like Florida and Hong Kong—I will argue that any one of these barriers could prevent public scholarship from taking hold in the culture of UNG, thereby undermining the future scholarly life and regional impact of the university.

Breaking the Mold: Public Scholarship for Accountability and Credibility

My first two degrees were in music composition and literature, with an emphasis on piano performance. Hence, I have long been fascinated by the division between "academic music" and "popular music" that, in many ways, corresponds with the divide between public writing and scholarly writing. In 1958, Milton Babbitt, a venerated professor of music composition at Princeton University, wrote a commentary for the popular magazine *High Fidelity* provocatively titled "Who Cares If You Listen?" In his article, Babbitt (1958/1998) dismissed the concerns of people who were concerned that the music composed at colleges and universities was unpleasant and largely ignored by the general public. Instead, he argued that the music composed by his colleagues had attained such a high level of theoretical sophistication— similar to that in fields like biology, mathematics, or philosophy—that it was impossibly difficult for non-experts to appreciate. Therefore, he extolled the "unprecedented divergence between contemporary serious music and its listeners" (p. 1306) and concluded that other composers interested in creating "complex, difficult, and problematical" music "would do [themselves] and [their] music an immediate and eventual service by total, resolute, and voluntary withdrawal from [the] public world to one of private performance" (p. 1310).

Babbitt's stance may seem extreme, but it resonated with music composers working at other universities. For example, Arnold Schoenberg (1975), a similarly influential composer at the University of California, Los Angeles, related a personal crisis concerning his music's belated popularity after World War II:

My works were played everywhere and acclaimed in such a manner that I started to doubt the value of my music . . . If previously my music had been difficult to understand on account of the peculiarities of my ideas and the way in which I expressed them, how could it happen that now, all of a sudden, everybody could follow my ideas and like them? Either the music or the audience was worthless. (p. 51)

Unfortunately, too many professors in academia are similarly comfortable with the idea that their scholarship—concealed behind expensive paywalls in scholarly journals and university press monographs—is hopelessly beyond the grasp of the general public. From the first day of PhD studies through the final days of tenure, professors tell themselves a comforting story: that truly groundbreaking scholarship is inevitably celebrated for its revelatory insights, but only amongst peers who have the scholarly background for deep appreciation.

To be clear, I believe strongly in the need for methodological rigor, theoretical advancement, and peer critique in academic scholarship. Nevertheless, colleges and universities today are consistently under attack for a perceived lack of accountability to the taxpayers who subsidize higher education (Erickson, 2019; Mintz, 2022). This lack of accountability is blamed for poor student outcomes and degrees that have questionable value in the labor market (Elliott & Jones, 2019; Koenig, 2022). Aside from this market-oriented perspective, other critics of higher education have argued that too many professors indulge in dubious research agendas that lack societal impact (e.g., Hess & LoGerfo, 2006; Holm et al., 2015).

I appreciate these critiques, but they are not caused by institutional waste, a disregard for student outcomes, or an epidemic of self-absorbed research agendas. If anything, all but the wealthiest U.S. colleges and universities have become remarkably lean institutions that feel tremendous pressure from policymakers and external funders to have a laser focus on student support and success, as well as impactful and entrepreneurial research (Kelderman, 2019; Mintz, 2021; Neitzel, 2020). Furthermore, attacks on researcher credibility and institutional accountability are not new to higher education (e.g., Heller, 2001) nor are they limited to the United States (e.g., Rhoades & Sporn, 2002). I would instead argue that the lack of trust evinced by the general public is directly related to higher education's inability to communicate the effectiveness of its values, scholarship, and student achievements. Patricia Limerick (1993), a professor of history and

Director for the Center of the American West at the University of Colorado, incisively skewered the state of scholarly discourse in the pages of the *New York Times*:

> In Colorado, as in most states, the legislators are convinced that the university is neglecting students and wasting state resources on pointless research. Under those circumstances, the miserable writing habits of professors pose a direct and concrete danger to higher education. Rather than going to the state legislature, proudly presenting stacks of the faculty's compelling and engaging publications, you end up hoping that the lawmakers stay out of the library and stay away, especially, from the periodical room, with its piles of academic journals. The habits of academic writers lend powerful support to the impression that research is a waste of the writers' time and of the public's money. (p. 201)

Even though this critique was written almost three decades ago, scholarly writing has remained largely esoteric and unappealing. With the exception of a few individuals, such as sociologist Matthew Desmond, higher education scholar Angel Jones, and theoretical physicist Michio Kaku, few professors have achieved success in translating their research and their discoveries to influence public policy and capture the public imagination. This is troubling for the future of higher education, as credibility is essential for universities to receive continued financial support from an increasingly skeptical political class—and for researchers to build public support and apply their expertise to solve the world's most intractable problems.

Barriers to Public Scholarship

Barrier 1: A Lack of Training

If public scholarship is so important for accountability and credibility, then why is it so difficult to produce? One primary barrier concerns the fact that few doctoral programs offer organized and dedicated training in public scholarship. Among those doctoral programs which do encourage students to engage in public outreach activities, the training is usually optional, offered at odd hours, and identified as a "low priority" in comparison to a student's lab work or scholarly journal writing. As David Labaree (2020), a widely respected Stanford University sociologist and historian of education, recently observed on his blog, "[professors] learn turgid writing in graduate school, as part of our induction into the profession, and we stay in this mode for the rest of our careers—long after we have lost the need to shore up our initially shaky credibility as serious scholars" (n.p.). This is a tragic state of affairs, as the aptitude to communicate and engage with varied audiences is not a natural skill. Similar to learning a musical instrument, writing for public audiences is a skill that is developed through continuous feedback and practice. Furthermore, in a multicultural world where an individual can leverage technology to communicate with global audiences, effective communication is essential to ensure that important discoveries are disseminated and correctly understood. Public communication along these lines can be tricky, however, especially if a scholar presumes that their job is to enlighten rather than to stimulate dialogue (Bennett & Jennings, 2011). Without practice, such engagement can come across as arrogant and tone-deaf, alienating the audience before dialogue can be facilitated.

UNG's doctoral program in Higher Education Leadership and Practice has deliberately attempted to break this cycle by encouraging graduate students to write in multiple genres and for different audiences. Hence, while they are completing their dissertation chapters, doctoral students also translate their research and accrued knowledge into multiple writing genres, including grant proposals, book reviews, op-eds, and other types of argumentative and persuasive essays. Through such writing exercises, students not only develop an awareness of their individual writing styles and biases but also learn to recognize that evidence marshaled in support of an author's arguments needs to be recognized as valid by their intended audience. At times, the word requirements of these writing assignments are deliberately short. The shortened word count gives students an appreciation for concise and accessible language, the elimination of jargon, and the value of multiple revisions. Faculty who arrive at UNG as early-career scholars would also benefit from similar training so that an institutional ethos of public scholarship and outreach can give UNG a distinctive edge over other regional universities. In short, intentional training that acknowledges systemic professional shortcomings in writing can address one significant barrier to public scholarship.

Barrier 2: Professional Incentives and Institutional Mission Creep

This leads to a second barrier: the professional incentives that currently exist for early-career scholars, as well as the institutional mission creep that encourages nearly every institution in the country to celebrate publication in a "prestigious academic journal" over publication in a magazine or website that may have a much broader readership. My own research frequently involves the study of organizational culture, so I have long been fascinated by how higher education institutions *signal* their organizational priorities to graduate students and newly hired professors (Tierney & Lanford, 2018a, 2018b). As part of their doctoral training, every graduate student is socialized into understanding the evaluative research criteria that haunt their given fields. These criteria have become increasingly commodified and based on quantitative measures, such as citation counts, h-indices, and journal rankings. Doctoral candidates who do not pay due attention to the hierarchy of journals when publishing their research are all too often considered "less attractive" on the faculty job market.

Even after attaining a coveted tenure-track position, one of the first important documents a professor receives is a comprehensive list of the institution's promotion and tenure guidelines. An institution's mission statement may extol the importance of public outreach and community engagement, but the promotion and tenure guidelines concerning research and scholarship almost invariably emphasize different criteria. At research-intensive institutions, professors quickly recognize that "success" is measured through grant money and publications in a select few prestigious journals. While these pressures may not be as intense at teaching-focused institutions like UNG, the widespread use of point systems for research assessment ensures that the hierarchy of scholarship is not simply maintained but made even more competitive and exclusionary over time.

Here is where I have to acknowledge my personal biases. One of the most attractive aspects of UNG, in my opinion, is the agency we have—particularly at this moment in the institution's development—to chart our own path. From an institutional perspective, I would encourage us to ask the following two questions:

What are our motivations for replicating such a hierarchy in our own faculty scholarship assessment practices? Do those practices correspond with our institutional aspirations and our mission?

Related to these questions, my work on institutional culture points to a couple areas of concern. First, the phenomenon of mission creep dictates that today's requirement of one or two journal articles usually becomes multiple articles as new peer institutions are identified—and a selective list of approved journals once the institution considers itself a research university. Second, my own research consistently illustrates that innovative colleges and universities do not mindlessly replicate the evaluative criteria of "peer" or "aspirant" institutions. They chart criteria coherent to their missions, and they grant talented people the agency to devise their own evaluative methods to determine quality and progress in their work. I would argue that this is the preferred path forward for UNG.

There is an additional question that needs to be addressed: What do our promotion and tenure criteria *signal* to prospective and new faculty we might hire, especially given our expressed desire to foster a more inclusive and diverse community?

Those of us who have been blessed to have a paper published by a peer-reviewed journal can certainly celebrate the fruits of our hard work, but we might also want to reflect on the privilege that facilitates our publications and the good fortune that allowed our research to be validated by a willing editor and reviewers. Sometimes, the double-blind, peer-review process functions as it is intended; it sharpens a scholar's work and exemplifies collegiality. All too often, however, the process is not entirely blind in fields of study where a select handful of individuals are experts nor is it a dialogue between peers of equal power and agency.

Even at its best, the peer review process is often far too slow for research to effectively impact practice (Jones, 2021). The faculty members who take on editor roles and review articles are not generally paid for their labor; hence, an article might take two, even three, years to progress from initial submission to publication. Furthermore, the process of peer review has all too often silenced excellent scholarship, especially by researchers from traditionally marginalized groups. To cite just one example, scholarship on Indigenous colleges remains practically non-existent in U.S. journals, yet it is an active and critical area of research in Canada and Australia.

Therefore, I believe UNG should think carefully about what we are signaling to a newly hired professor whose research agenda embraces an area of their discipline that has been unjustly ignored because it does not readily lead to major grants. We should carefully consider our signals to a new professor who would like to employ new theoretical frameworks to solve a particularly difficult problem—or our signals to a professor with enviable multidisciplinary expertise but whose scholarship does not comfortably fit the aims and scope of siloed journals. These scholars may be innovators who will integrate ideas from different fields of study and make a substantive contribution that impacts daily life and excites the general public (Tierney & Lanford, 2016). Unfortunately, such scholars are rarely hired at research-intensive universities today, as they are focused on the narrow scholarly criteria that determine academic prestige. It is my hope that such innovative scholars would be welcomed and supported at UNG.

Barrier No. 3: The Dismantling of Academic Freedom and Tenure

A third barrier concerns the unfortunate dismantling of academic freedom and tenure throughout the United States. As I have written in previous articles for audiences in Australia, China, Europe, and India (e.g., Lanford, 2021a; Lanford & Tierney, 2016; Tierney & Lanford, 2014, 2015), U.S. colleges and universities have staunchly defended the concept of academic freedom for over a century, since the 1915 formation of the American Association of University Professors (AAUP) by a coalition of professors led by John Dewey. Their stance was that "the professoriate [needed] a significant degree of autonomy in the manner in which they conduct their work in order to have the freedom of thought and expression that is seen as necessary to advance knowledge and learning" (Tierney, 2001, p. 9). Over time, their position has been affirmed by the unbelievable vitality and research productivity of contemporary U.S. higher education. Whereas not one U.S. university would likely have been considered a top

100 institution in 1915, more than half of the world's top 50 universities today are located in the United States (Clotfelter, 2019).

One of the great benefits of living abroad is how it can encourage reflection on the cultural beliefs and norms that an individual takes for granted concerning their home culture. Similarly, when talking with international audiences, the unique features of the U.S. higher education system are highlighted in ways an individual rarely considers at home. For example, the notion of "academic freedom" seems like a beautiful dream in an environment where professors are being imprisoned, or even subject to death, due to research that interrogates systemic inequalities, raises uncomfortable questions about the unlawful actions of entrenched corporate interests, or sheds a light on unjust actions by authoritarian governments.

However, I think we make a fatal error if we assume that the political environments of places like Turkey, Hong Kong, France, Denmark, and other countries where academic freedom has come under severe attack in recent years are so different from ours. When I studied and worked at the University of Hong Kong from 2010 to 2012, I would argue that academic discourse was more vibrant—and academic freedom better protected—than it currently is in many areas of the United States. Around 2015, however, Hong Kong media and political figures started to ask for information about course content in the university system. They publicly criticized professors who spread "separatist" and "unpatriotic" ideas, similar to what we have seen in the United States in recent years. No one was explicitly "censored," as academic freedom is rarely threatened by overt censorship. Over time, though, policies concerning tenure and promotion were changed, and professors who wrote about societal inequities, historical inaccuracies, and vested corporate interests were simply fired under the pretense that their scholarship was not "world class."

Academic freedom in the United States is similarly under attack today by multiple actors. Politicians and policymakers regularly attempt to stifle informed criticism by professors who can back their arguments with empirical data and disciplinary expertise. Wealthy and powerful individuals attack critical theories which simply question prevailing norms, values, and institutions, concerned that the enlarged discourse which might spring from such interrogation will threaten their privileged standing. Corporate entities contend that higher education should be entirely privatized, focusing on the transmission of knowledge to develop skills deemed important in the labor market rather than on the cultivation of innovative ideas which stimulate humanistic inquiry and scientific progress and the development of informed citizens who can thoughtfully contribute to a democratic society.

Barma and Goldgeier (2022) have cogently demonstrated that scholars who identify with one or more minoritized groups and engage with social media are frequent targets for their scholarship and their informed analyses:

> [They are] often met with forms of bullying, public trolling, and harassment that impose deeply troubling individual and social costs. Some may simply decide it's not worth it and stop engaging. University leadership, often eager for their faculty to engage with the public and policy communities for the visibility that provides, must be committed to helping faculty facing online harassment and bullying to manage these harrowing situations. (p. 1774)

In regions of the world where academic freedom is weak or not protected, faculty are particularly vulnerable to repugnant attacks (Shahvisi, 2021). These types of attacks could severely damage the strides UNG has made toward greater diversity and inclusion, global engagement through military programs, global learning on UNG campuses, and international recruitment—each of which are detailed extensively in this volume (Antonia et al., 2023; Dawson et al., 2023; Namatovu et al., 2023; Schulte et al., 2023). Hence, one could reasonably argue that academic freedom is an even more vital tenet of higher education in a 21st century environment where so much of local and global public discourse transpires in social media spaces. If institutions are loathe to openly defend scholars' right to conduct research and teach in a manner congruent with their professional expertise, social media can become a mechanism for the subjugation of individual professors, rather than a platform where faculty can freely engage with local communities and share their unique insights and new ideas with a globalized society. Moreover, as noted by Ariel Turner and Bonita

Jacobs (2023) in this volume, "successful town/gown relationships require openness, transparency, and continued discussion about how one works with the other." Therefore, without academic freedom, the conditions necessary for transparent engagement and open dialogue among community leaders, university leadership, and faculty would be severely curtailed (Adams & Lanford, 2021).

The changes in tenure policies that are rapidly being proposed throughout the country are equally damaging. Tenure provides the structural protection under which academic freedom can be exercised. Theoretically, tenured professors can speak against a policy related to their expertise, the manner in which curricula in their disciplines are designed, or a statement made by a prominent university official, and, due to tenure, they should not be threatened with the loss of their job (Tierney & Lanford, 2014). In an environment where tenure protections have been weakened, however, few professors will engage in public scholarship that brings attention to their work and their expertise. The potential for pushback from powerful external forces would be too great, and the result would be a neutered academic environment where important findings would be withheld and dissenting voices, no matter how well informed or justified, would be silenced. Through the dismantling of academic freedom and tenure, the United States would relinquish the single greatest advantage it has for the stimulation of scientific production and innovation—and community-oriented universities dedicated to student development and regional entrepreneurship, like UNG, would incur the greatest harm.

Conclusion

In conclusion, I believe it is not enough to merely incentivize public scholarship through extrinsic rewards (although such rewards are certainly welcome). It is incumbent for UNG to strategically make public scholarship part of the mission of the university, socialize students and faculty to the importance of public outreach, embed public scholarship in graduate student and faculty development, and continuously evaluate information channels through which public scholarship can be disseminated and promoted. These goals are even more important if UNG's stated intention is to encourage diverse voices, produce innovative scholarship, speak with different audiences beyond the academy, and raise vital questions about economic developments and policies that are impacting the North Georgia region. Even though many higher education institutions have long paid lip service to the importance of public scholarship (e.g., Boyer, 1990), my belief is that UNG could be a leader in the field of public scholarship— charting an exciting course for societal engagement that differs from the well-trod path of exclusivity many aspiring research universities have thoughtlessly traversed. Furthermore, UNG must lead by affirming the principles of academic freedom and tenure and making a commitment to protect scholars who courageously choose to work with marginalized communities, engage the public, and ensure that their research has a palpable impact on society. In my own work, I am making a commitment to produce at least one piece of public scholarship for every paper I publish in a scholarly journal or university press book. In short, I am attempting to honor Terra's question and do better to create change, and I believe we—as a community of teachers, scholars, and leaders at UNG—can continue to improve as well.

References

Adams, K. A., & Lanford, M. (2021). Reimagining global partnerships in higher education through open systems theory. *Journal of International and Comparative Higher Education, 13*(5), 108–123.

Babbitt, M. (1998). Who cares if you listen? In O. Strunk (Ed.), *Source readings in music history* (pp. 1305–1310). Norton. Reprinted from *High Fidelity, 8*(2), 38–40, 126–127.

Barma, N. H., & Goldgeier, J. (2022). How not to bridge the gap in international relations. *International Affairs, 98*(5), 1763–1781. https://doi.org/10.1093/ia/iiac102

Bennett, D. J., & Jennings, R. C. (2011). (Eds.). *Successful science communication: Telling it like it is*. Cambridge University Press.

Boyer, E. (1990). *Scholarship reconsidered: Priorities of the professoriate*. Princeton University Press.

Clotfelter, C. T. (2019). *Big-time sports in American universities* (2nd ed.).

Cambridge University Press.

Elliott, K., & Jones, T. (2019, September 19). *Creating accountability for college access and success: Recommendations for the Higher Education Act and beyond*. Education Trust. https://edtrust.org/resource/creating-accountability-for-college-access-and-success-recommendations-for-the-higher-education-act-and-beyond/

Erickson, L. (2019). College administrators support greater accountability in higher education. *Third Way*. https://www.thirdway.org/polling/college-administrators-support-greater-accountability-in-higher-ed

Heller, D. E. (2001). Introduction: The changing dynamics of affordability, access, and accountability in public higher education. In D. E. Heller (Ed.), *The states and public higher education policy: Affordability, access, and accountability* (pp. 1–10). Johns Hopkins University Press.

Hess, F. M., & LoGerfo, L. (2006, May 8). Chicanas from outer space: Educational research is an education! *National Review*. https://www.nationalreview.com/article/217519/chicanas-outer-space-frederick-m-hess-laura-logerfo

Holm, P., Jarrick, A., & Scott, D. (2015). *Humanities world report 2015*. Palgrave Macmillan.

Jones, A. M. (2021, April 6). Academe should value the impact factor of public scholarship. *Inside Higher Ed*. https://www.insidehighered.com/advice/2021/04/06/higher-ed-should-value-impact-public-scholarship-through-social-media-opinion

Kelderman, E. (2019). *The rise of performance-based funding: How colleges are adapting in the new age of accountability*. Chronicle of Higher Education. https://www.luminafoundation.org/wp-content/uploads/2019/05/performance-based-funding.pdf

Koenig, R. (2022, March 28). Making higher ed more accountable for student job outcomes. *EdSurge*. https://www.edsurge.com/news/2022-03-28-making-higher-ed-more-accountable-for-student-job-outcomes

Labaree, D. (2020, April 20). Patricia Limerick: Dancing with professors. *David Labaree on schooling, history, and writing*. https://davidlabaree.com/2020/04/20/limerick-dancing-with-professors/

Lanford, M. (2019). Making sense of "outsiderness": How life history informs the college experiences of non-traditional students. *Qualitative Inquiry, 25*(5), 500–512. https://doi.org/10.1177/1077800418817839

Lanford, M. (2020). What can relational sociology reveal about college writing and remediation? In W. G. Tierney & S. Kolluri (Eds.), *Relational sociology and research on schools, colleges, and universities* (pp. 157–180). State University of New York Press.

Lanford, M. (2021a). Critical perspectives on global partnerships in higher education: Strategies for inclusion, social impact, and effectiveness. *Journal of International and Comparative Education, 13*(5), 10–14. https://ojed.org/index.php/jcihe/article/view/4449

Lanford, M. (2021b). Institutional competition through performance funding: A catalyst or hindrance to teaching and learning? *Educational Philosophy and Theory, 53*(11), 1148–1160. https://doi.org/10.1080/00131857.2020.1783246

Lanford, M., & Tierney, W. G. (2016). The international branch campus: Cloistered community or agent of social change? In D. Neubauer, J. Hawkins, M. Lee, & C. Collins (Eds.), *The Palgrave handbook of Asia Pacific higher education* (pp. 157–172). Palgrave Macmillan. https://doi.org/10.1057/978-1-137-48739-1_11

Lanford, M., & Tierney, W. G. (2022). *Creating a culture of mindful innovation in higher education.* SUNY Press.

Limerick, P. N. (1993, October 31). Dancing with professors: The trouble with academic prose. *New York Times Book Review*, 3, 23–24.

Mintz, B. (2021). Neoliberalism and the crisis in higher education: The cost of ideology. *American Journal of Economics and Sociology, 80*(1), 79–112. https://doi.org/10.1111/ajes.12370

Mintz, S. (2022, January 5). The need for greater accountability in higher education. *Inside Higher Ed.* https://www.insidehighered.com/blogs/higher-ed-gamma/need-greater-accountability-higher-education

Nietzel, M. T. (2020, January 9). Gates foundation launches major student success initiative. *Forbes.* https://www.forbes.com/sites/michaeltnietzel/2020/01/09/gates-foundation-launches-major-student-success-initiative/?sh=71b6ff70bbf8

Rhoades, G., & Sporn, B. (2002). Quality assurance in Europe and the U.S.: Professional and political economic framing of higher education policy. *Higher Education, 43*(3), 355–390.

Shahvisi, A. (2021). On the social epistemology of academic freedom. In R. Dutt-Ballerstadt & K. Bhattacharya (Eds.), *Civility, free speech, and academic freedom in higher education: Faculty on the margins* (pp. 59–71). Routledge.

Tierney, W. G. (2001). Academic freedom and organizational identity. *Australian Universities' Review, 44*, 7–14.

Tierney, W. G., & Lanford, M. (2014). The question of academic freedom: Universal right or relative term? *Frontiers of Education in China, 9*(1), 4–23. https://doi.org/10.1007/BF03396999

Tierney, W. G., & Lanford, M. (2015). An investigation of the impact of international branch campuses on organizational culture. *Higher Education, 70*(2), 283–298. https://doi.org/10.1007/s10734-014-9845-7

Tierney, W. G., & Lanford, M. (2016). Creativity and innovation in the twenty-first century university. In J. M. Case & J. Huisman (Eds.), *Researching higher education: International perspectives on theory, policy, and practice* (pp. 61–79). Society for Research into Higher Education. Routledge.

Tierney, W. G., & Lanford, M. (2018a). Institutional culture in higher education. In J. C. Shin & P. N. Teixeira (Eds.), *Encyclopedia of international higher education systems and institutions* (pp. 1–9). Springer. https://doi.org/10.1007/978-94-017-9553-1_544-1

Tierney, W. G., & Lanford, M. (2018b). Research in higher education: Cultural perspectives. In J. C. Shin & P. N. Teixeira (Eds.), *Encyclopedia of international higher education systems and institutions* (pp. 1–6). Springer. https://doi.org/10.1007/978-94-017-9553-1_165-1

INDEX

CPSIA information can be obtained
at www.ICGtesting.com
Printed in the USA
JSHW071407080223
37403JS00010B/65